# Langenscheidt

# Spotlights

Englische und amerikanische Kurzgeschichten
mit Wortschatzhilfen

W0191205

**Langenscheidt**

Berlin · München · Wien · Zürich · New York

© 2003 Langenscheidt KG, Berlin und München
Druck: Druckhaus Langenscheidt, Berlin-Schöneberg
Printed in Germany
ISBN 3-468-44424-9
www.langenscheidt.de

3. 4. 5. * 07 06 05 04

# Vorwort

"Spotlights" enthält Kurzgeschichten mit aktuellen und zur persönlichen Stellungnahme herausfordernden Themen. Im „Scheinwerferlicht" stehen Rassendiskriminierung, Emanzipation, Leistungsgesellschaft, soziale Gleichheit, wissenschaftlicher Fortschritt.

Aber auch einige der großen zeitlosen Probleme wie die Tragik des Alterns, das Verhältnis von Jugend und Alter, Partnerschaft in der Ehe finden wir im „Rampenlicht" dieser Erzählungen. Die Namen der Verfasser verbürgen den hohen literarischen Wert der Geschichten.

Wie bei den anderen Bändchen dieser Reihe wurden die schwierigen englischen Wörter fett gedruckt und ihre Übersetzungen in den Fußnoten aufgeführt, sodass sich das Buch sehr gut zur Erweiterung vorhandener und zur Auffrischung vergessener Sprachkenntnisse eignet.

Langenscheidt

*Wir danken folgenden Verlagen, Agenturen und Autoren bzw. deren Rechtsnachfolgern für die Abdruckgenehmigungen:*

Liberty Library Corporation, New York, für "Spotlight" von Budd Schulberg. Copyright © 1978 by Liberty Library Corporation.

Linder AG, Literarische Agenturen, Zürich, für "The Weapon" von Fredric Brown. Copyright © 1951 by Street and Smith Publications Incorporated for Astounding Magazine.

Irwin Shaw für "The Girls in Their Summer Dresses".

The New Yorker für "The Test" von Angelica Gibbs. Copyright © 1940, 1968 The New Yorker Magazine, Inc. Henry Slesar für "Examination Day". Originally appeared in Playboy Magazine. Copyright © 1958 by Henry Slesar.

Intercontinental Literary Agency. London, für "The Pedestrian" von Ray Bradbury, "The Chaser" von John Collier und "Inexperience" von Frank Tuohy.

Mrs. James Thurber für "The Unicorn in the Garden" von James Thurber. Copyright © 1940 James Thurber. Copyright © 1968 Helen Thurber. From "Fables of our Time", Published by Harper & Row, New York. Originally printed in The New Yorker.

A.P. Watt Ltd, Literary Agents, London, für "News of the Engagement" aus "The Grim Smile of the Five Towns" von Arnold Bennett und "Dr Abraham" aus "The Moon and Sixpence" von William Somerset Maugham. Copyright © Estate of the Late Arnold Bennett und Copyright © Estate of the Late William Somerset Maugham.

A.D. Peters & Co Ltd, Writers' Agents, London, für "The Snob" von Moreley Callaghan.

The Society of Authors as literary representative of the Estate of James Joyce für "Eveline" aus "The Dubliners" von James Joyce.

Laurence Pollinger Limited, Authors' Agents, London, für "I Spy" von Graham Greene aus "Collected Stories" (The Bodley Head and William Heinemann).

The Bodley Head, London, für "My Financial Career" aus "Literary Lapses" von Stephen Leacock.

# Inhaltsverzeichnis

Die ersten acht Kurzgeschichten sind amerikanischer Herkunft. In ihnen wird daher die Schreibung des amerikanischen Englisch bevorzugt.

## Verwendete Abkürzungen

| | |
|---|---|
| AE | amerikanisches Englisch |
| *amer.* | amerikanisch |
| BE | britisches Englisch |
| *dial.* | Dialektform |
| *e-e* | eine |
| *e-n* | einen |
| *e-r* | einer |
| *e-s* | eines |
| *engl.* | englisch |
| *et.* | etwas |
| F | familiär (= Umgangssprache) |
| *franz.* | französisch |
| *Ggs.* | Gegensatz |
| *j-d* | jemand |
| *j-m* | jemandem |
| *j-n* | jemanden |
| *j-s* | jemandes |
| *männl.* | männlich |
| o.s. | oneself |
| *Pl* | Plural |
| *poet.* | dichterisch |
| *s-e* | seine |
| *s-n* | seinen |
| *s-r* | seiner |
| *s-s* | seines |
| *Sg* | Singular |
| *sl.* | Slang |
| s.o. | someone |
| *sog.* | so genannt |
| s.th. | something |
| u. | und |
| *weibl.* | weiblich |

# Erklärung der Lautschrift

## A    Vokale und Diphthonge

[ɑ:]    reines langes a, wie in Vater, kam, Schwan: *far* [fɑ:], *father* ['fɑ:ðə].

[ʌ]    kommt im Deutschen nicht vor. Kurzes dunkles a, bei dem die Lippen nicht gerundet sind. Vorn und offen gebildet: *butter* ['bʌtə], *come* [kʌm], *colour* ['kʌlə], *blood* [blʌd], *flourish* ['flʌrɪʃ], *twopence* ['tʌpəns].

[æ]    heller, ziemlich offener, nicht zu kurzer a-Laut wie das kurze a in Quatsch, waschen: *fat* [fæt], *man* [mæn].

[eə]    nicht zu offenes halb langes ä; im Englischen nur vor r, das als ein dem ä nachhallendes ə erscheint: *bare* [beə], *pair* [peə], *there* [ðeə].

[aɪ]    Bestandteile: helles, zwischen ɑ: und æ liegendes a und schwächeres offenes i. Die Zunge hebt sich halbwegs zur i-Stellung: *I* [aɪ], *lie* [laɪ], *dry* [draɪ].

[aʊ]    Bestandteile: helles, zwischen ɑ: und æ liegendes a und schwächeres offenes u: *house* [haʊs, *now* [naʊ].

[eɪ]    halb offenes e, nach i auslautend, indem die Zunge sich halbwegs zur i-Stellung hebt: *date* [deɪt], *play* [pleɪ], *obey* [ə'beɪ].

[e]    halb offenes kurzes e, etwas geschlossener als das e in Bett: *bed* [bed], *less* [les].

[ə]    flüchtiger Gleitlaut, ähnlich dem deutschen, flüchtig gesprochenen e in Gelage: *about* [ə'baʊt], *butter* ['bʌtə], *connect* [kə'nekt].

[i:]    langes i, wie in lieb, Bibel, aber etwas offener einsetzend als im Deutschen; wird in Südengland doppellautig gesprochen, indem sich die Zunge allmählich zur i-Stellung hebt: *scene* [si:n], *sea* [si:], *feet* [fi:t], *ceiling* ['si:lɪŋ].

[ɪ]    kurzes offenes i wie in bin, mit: *big* [bɪg], *city* ['sɪtɪ].

[ɪə]    halb offenes halb langes i mit nachhallendem ə: *here* [hɪə], *hear* [hɪə], *inferior* [ɪn'fɪərɪə].

[əʊ]  mit [ə] beginnend und in schwaches u auslautend, keine Rundung der Lippen, kein Heben der Zunge: *note* [nəʊt], *boat* [bəʊt], *below* [bɪ'ləʊ].

[ɔː]  offener langer, zwischen a und o schwebender Laut: *fall* [fɔːl], *nought* [nɔːt], *or* [ɔː], *before* [bɪ'fɔː].

[ɒ]  offener kurzer, zwischen a und o schwebender Laut, offener als das o in Motte: *god* [gɒd], *not* [nɒt], *wash* [wɒʃ], *hobby* ['hɒbɪ].

[ɔɪ]  Bestandteile: offenes o und schwächeres offenes i. Die Zunge hebt sich halbwegs zur i-Stellung: *voice* [vɔɪs], *boy* [bɔɪ], *annoy* [ə'nɔɪ].

[ɜː]  im Deutschen fehlender Laut; offenes langes ö, etwa wie gedehnt gesprochenes ö in öffnen, Mörder; kein Vorstülpen oder Runden der Lippen; kein Heben der Zunge: *word* [wɜːd], *girl* [gɜːl], *learn* [lɜːn], *murmur* ['mɜːmə].

[uː]  langes u wie in Buch, doch ohne Lippenrundungen; vielfach diphthongisch als halb offenes langes u mit nachhallendem geschlossenem u: *fool* [fuːl], *shoe* [ʃuː], *you* [juː], *rule* [ruːl], *canoe* [kə'nuː].

[ʊə]  halb offenes halb langes u mit nachhallendem ə: *poor* [pʊə], *sure* [ʃʊə]], *allure* [ə'ljʊə].

[ʊ]  flüchtiges u: *put* [pʊt], *look* [lʊk], *careful* ['keəfʊl].

Die **Länge eines Vokals** wird durch [ː] bezeichnet, z.B. *ask* [ɑːsk], *astir* [ə'stɜː]. Die **Betonung** der englischen Wörter wird durch das Zeichen ['] vor der zu betonenden Silbe angegeben, z.B. *onion* ['ʌnjən].

## B    Konsonanten

[r]    nur vor Vokalen gesprochen. Völlig verschieden vom deutschen Zungenspitzen- oder Zäpfchen-r. Die Zungenspitze bildet mit der oberen Zahnwulst eine Enge, durch die der Ausatmungsstrom mit Stimmton hindurchgetrieben wird, ohne den Laut zu rollen. Am Ende eines Wortes wird r nur bei Bindung mit dem Anlautvokal des folgenden Wortes gesprochen; *rose* [rəʊz], *pride* [praɪd], *there is* [ðeər'ɪz].

[ʒ]    stimmhaftes sch, wie g in Genie, j in Journal: *azure* ['æʒə], *jazz* [dʒæz], *jeep* [dʒiːp], *large* [lɑːdʒ].

[ʃ]    stimmloses sch, wie im Deutschen Schnee, rasch: *shake* [ʃeɪk], *washing* ['wɒʃɪŋ], *lash* [læʃ].

[θ]    im Deutschen nicht vorhandener stimmloser Lispellaut; durch Anlegen der Zunge an die oberen Schneidezähne hervorgebracht: *thin* [θɪn], *path* [pɑːθ], *method* ['meθəd].

[ð]    derselbe Laut stimmhaft, d.h. mit Stimmton: *there* [ðeə], *breathe* [briːð], *father* ['fɑːðə].

[s]    stimmloser Zischlaut, entsprechend dem deutschen ß in Spaß, reißen: *see* [siː], *hats* [hæts], *decide* [dɪ'saɪd].

[z]    stimmhafter Zischlaut wie im Deutschen sausen: *zeal* [ziːl], *rise* [raɪz], *horizon* [hə'raɪzn].

[ŋ]    wird wie der deutsche Nasenlaut in fangen, singen gebildet: *ring* [rɪŋ], *singer* ['sɪŋə].

[ŋk]   derselbe Laut mit nachfolgendem k wie im Deutschen senken, Wink: *ink* [ɪŋk], *tinker* ['tɪŋkə].

[w]    flüchtiges, mit Lippe an Lippe gesprochenes w, aus der Mundstellung für uː gebildet: *will* [wɪll], *swear* [sweə], *queen* [kwiːn].

[f]    stimmloser Lippenlaut wie im Deutschen flott: *fat* [fæt], *tough* [tʌf], *effort* ['efət].

[v]    stimmhafter Lippenlaut wie im Deutschen Vase, Ventil: *vein* [veɪn], *velvet* ['velvɪt].

[j]    flüchtiger zwischen j und i schwebender Laut: *onion* ['ʌnjən], *yes* [jes], *filial* ['fɪljəl].

# Spotlight

*Budd Schulberg*

The **director** was trying to bring the **picture** through in twenty-nine days. The assistant director was trying to impress the director. The second assistant was trying to prove his right to be a first assistant. The three hundred **extras** were trying to please everybody. The ten-dollar people were trying to fight their way into focus. The seven-and-a-halfs were walking **briskly** back and forth, **doing their perspiring be**st.

'All right, **folks**, get *moving!*' the second assistant screamed. 'Now watch me. When I wave this handkerchief, start walking as if you expected to get somewhere.'

'What're ya watching him for?' the first assistant yelled. 'When *I* drop my hand, **start talking it up**. You're all happy, see? And make it good! **We gotta finish** by six sharp.'

The director, **running sweat**, sleeves rolled up, **paced** impatiently. 'What's the trouble, boys?' he barked. 'I'm half a day behind now. **Get the lead out**.'

It was another of those **scorching** Hollywood afternoons. One of those **tough**, irritable days. The extras had been at it since nine that morning. When the long-awaited **recess** came, they crowded around the **water cooler**.

'After you,' a **florid**-faced, whitehaired old man offered politely. When he was almost trampled in the rush, he took his place philosophically at the end of the line. He **mopped**

---

**spotlight** ['spɒtlaɪt] Scheinwerfer-, Rampenlicht, Schlaglicht
**director** [dɪ'rektə] Regisseur  **picture** ['pɪktʃə] Film  **extra** ['ekstrə] Statist  **brisk** [brɪsk] lebhaft  **doing their perspiring best** [pə'spaɪərɪŋ] (und) taten schwitzend ihr Bestes  **folk** [fəʊks] Leute
**Start talking it up** AE Raus mit der Sprache!  **we gotta finish** AE F ['gɒtə] = we (have) got to finish  **running sweat** [swet] schweiß-überströmt  **pace** [peɪs] hin- und hergehen  **Get the lead out** [led] Bewegt euch nicht so bleiern!  **scorching** ['skɔːtʃɪŋ] glühend heiß
**tough** [tʌf] hart, schwer  **recess** [rɪ'ses] Pause  **water cooler** Trinkbrunnen  **florid** ['flɒrɪd] rosig, blühend  **mop** [mɒp] wischen

his face professionally with an edge of his handkerchief. His calm silence was like a wall of glass cutting him off from the **whirlpool** of excitement all around him.

Even at the call, 'Take your places, everybody,' he displayed not the slightest trace of emotion. He **straightened** the **dress suit** he wore and took his place in the line again.

When the director said, 'Pick me out some people for **flash reactions**,' excitement stirred the crowd. For some it might mean the chance they had waited and struggled for. For others it meant the extra fifteen dollars they would earn if they were asked to speak a line.

As the old man saw the assistant director **descending on** him, he waited **docilely**, like an old horse about to be saddled. But he wasn't sure he wanted this unexpected momentary spotlight. He was old and tired, and this meant strong lights in his eyes and the **strain** of having to learn new words and speak them within the next few minutes.

But even as he hoped the assistant wasn't going to **single** him **out** for a **close-up**, he was praying that he would. Because extra work had become scarcer and scarcer through the summer; his last job had been two ten-dollar days three weeks ago. That meant **pressing** the dress suit yourself, and **stalling** the **landlady**. Now this additional fifteen dollars would be the difference between keeping the room and packing up again.

Then the assistant was on him. 'All right, **Pop**, we'll use you.' He stepped into the **glare**, waiting quietly with eyes half closed as the director opened up on him.

---

**whirlpool** ['wɜːlpuːl] Wirbel, Strudel    **straighten** ['streɪtn] hier: glatt streichen    **dress suit** ['dress 'sjuːt] Frack    **flash reaction** hier: Einzelaufnahme    **descend on** [dɪ'send] sich stürzen auf    **docile** ['dəʊsaɪl] gefügig    **strain** [streɪn] Anstrengung    **single out** ['sɪŋgl] auswählen    **close-up** ['kləʊsʌp] Nah-, Großaufnahme    **press** bügeln    **stall** [stɔːl] vertrösten    **landlady** ['lænleɪdɪ] Hauswirtin, Zimmervermieterin    **pop** F [pɒp] Opa    **glare** [gleə] grelles Licht

'Okay, old-timer. This'll all be over in a minute—we hope. All you've got to do is smile and say, 'I've been waiting here thirty years for this,' and he gives you the **cue**. 'On this very spot?' and **then you give it this**—watch me.' And the director turned his head toward the floor and then quickly looked up again with an unexpected change of expression. 'Get it? Just a different version of that old **double take**.'

The old man nodded his head slowly. He said he thought he got it.

'Then let's go. See if we can't **get it in the can** the first time,' the director said, as the **juicers** hit the lights. He **crouched** below the cameras, watching the old man critically.

'**Hold it. Cut!**' he yelled. 'You forgot that double take. Try it again.'

More nervously, the old man tried again. 'I've been thirty years—'

'**For Pete's sake**! You forgot *'waiting'*! Waiting—what you're making us do! Take it once more.'

The old man nodded, wetting his lips, trembling. He began again. And again. The director **fumed** internally. Typical studio **economy**! Trying to save money with a ten-**buck** extra instead of paying an actor to do it! The old man **fumbled** the scene worse each time. He was trying too hard.

'Look, **pal**. You're making it too tough for yourself. It's just one quick **take**, see? Just that famous old trick with your eyes and a turn of your head. The thing what's-his-name, Willie

---

**cue** [kjuː] Stichwort   **then you give it this** dann machen Sie Folgendes   **double take** AE F ['dʌbl 'teɪk] hier: plötzlicher Wechsel des Gesichtsausdrucks, wenn „der Groschen fällt"   **get it in the can** hier: es hinkriegen   **juicer** AE sl. ['dʒuːsə] Beleuchter   **crouch** [kraʊtʃ] sich ducken   **Hold it. Cut!** Bleiben Sie so! Stopp!   **For Pete's sake!** [fə 'piːts 'seɪk] Um Himmels willen! Herrgott noch mal! **fume** [fjuːm] hier: „kochen"   **economy** [ɪ'kɒnəmɪ] Sparmaßnahme **buck** AE sl. [bʌk] Dollar   **fumble** ['fʌmbl] verpatzen   **pal** [pæl] Kamerad, Kumpel   **take** Szene, Aufnahme

Robbins, **originated** in the old **silent days**. Think you can do it?'

'I—I think I can do it now,' the old man said.

Everybody **hushed** again. The cameras started rolling. He made one more **tentative stab** at it. In vain.

'All right!' the director roared. 'Get back in the crowd— we'll try somebody else.'

And as the old man tried to disappear **inconspicuously**, he heard the director say, 'For heaven's sake get someone who knows what a double take is!' And an eager, **confident** extra took his place in the scene.

Back in the crowd of extras, he stood watching his successor. Just in front of him a **dumpy** elderly woman, one of the visitors to the **set**, was approaching the handsome young star with her **autograph** book opened. In a kind of reflex action, the star smiled and reached out for the book. But she had already gone by him! The old man looked up at her in surprise.

'I never thought I'd actually meet you—after all these years,' she said, and she held up the book.

For a moment he stared at her unbelievingly, and then, as he took the book and began to write in it, he seemed to grow broader and taller. He wrote silently, 'As ever, Willie Robbins,' handed the book back with a **faint** smile, and turned to watch the successful completion of the scene.

8.3.2006 (2x)

---

**originate** [əˈrɪɡʒɪneɪt] hier: erfinden   **silent days** [ˈsaɪlənt] Stummfilmzeit   **hush** [hʌʃ] verstummen   **tentative stab** [ˈtentətɪv] zaghafter Versuch   **inconspicuous** [ɪnkənˈspɪkjʊəs] unauffällig
**confident** [ˈkɒnfɪdənt] selbstsicher   **dumpy** [ˈdʌmpɪ] untersetzt
**set** Szenenaufbau   **autograph** [ˈɔːtəɡrɑːf] Autogramm   **faint** [feɪnt] leise, fein

# The Weapon

*Fredric Brown*

The room was quiet in the **dimness** of early evening. Dr James Graham, **key scientist** of a very important project, sat in his favorite chair, thinking. It was so still that he could hear the turning of pages in the next room as his son **leafed** through a picture book.

Often Graham did his best work, his most creative thinking, under these circumstances, sitting alone in an unlighted room in his own apartment after the day's regular work. But tonight his mind would not work constructively. Mostly he thought about his **mentally arrested** son—his only son—in the next room. The thoughts were loving thoughts, not the bitter **anguish** he had felt years ago when he had first learned of the boy's condition. The boy was happy; wasn't that the main thing? And to how many men is given a child who will always be a child, who will not grow up to leave him? Certainly that was **rationalization**, but what is wrong with rationalization when—The doorbell rang.

Graham rose and turned on lights in the almost-dark room before he went throuh the hallway to the door. He was not annoyed; tonight, at this moment, almost any interruption to his thoughts was welcome.

---

**weapon** ['wepən] Waffe    **dimness** ['dɪmnɪs] Dämmerung
**key scientist** ['kiː'saɪəntɪst] maßgebender Wissenschaftler    **leaf** [liːf]
blättern    **mentally arrested** ['mentəlɪ ə'restɪd] geistig zurück-
geblieben    **anguish** ['æŋgwɪʃ] Qual, Schmerz    **rationalization**
[ræʃnəlaɪ'zeɪʃn] intellektueller Selbstbetrug

He opened the door. A stranger stood there; he said, 'Dr Graham? My name is Niemand; I'd like to talk to you. May I come in a moment?'

Graham looked at him. He was as small man, **nondescript**, obviously harmless—possibly a reporter or an insurance agent.

But it didn't matter what he was. Graham found himself saying, 'Of course. Come in, Mr Niemand.' A few minutes of conversation, he **justified himself by thinking**, might **divert** his thoughts and clear his mind.

'Sit down,' he said, in the living room. 'Care for a drink?'

Niemand said, 'No, thank you.' He sat in the chair; Graham sat on the sofa.

The small man **interlocked** his fingers; he leaned forward. He said, 'Dr Graham, you are the man whose scientific work is more likely than that of any other man to end the human race's chance for **survival**.'

A **crackpot**, Graham thought. Too late now he realized that he should have asked the man's business before admitting him. It would be an **embarrassing** interview—he disliked being rude, yet only rudeness was effective.

'Dr Graham, the weapon on which you are working—'

The visitor stopped and turned his head as the door that led to a bedroom opened and a boy of fifteen came in. The boy didn't notice Niemand; he ran to Graham.

'Daddy, will you read to me now?' The boy of fifteen laughed the sweet laughter of a child of four.

---

**nondescript** ['nɒndɪskrɪpt] schwer einzuordnen   **he justified himself by thinking** dachte er zu s-r Rechtfertigung   **divert** [daɪ'vɜːt] ablenken   **interlock** [ɪntə'lɒk] ineinander verschränken   **survival** [sə'vaɪvəl] Überleben   **crackpot** ['krækpɒt] Spinner   **embarrassing** [ɪm'bærəsɪŋ] peinlich

Graham put an arm around the boy. He looked at his visitor, wondering whether he had known about the boy. From the lack of surprise on Niemand's face, Graham felt sure he had known.

'Harry'—Graham's voice was warm with **affection**—'Daddy's busy. Just for a little while. Go back to your room; I'll come and read to you soon.'

*'Chicken Little?* You'll read me *Chicken Little?'*

'If you wish. Now run along. Wait. Harry, this is Mr Niemand.'

The boy smiled **bashfully** at the visitor. Niemand said, 'Hi, Harry,' and smiled back at him, holding out his hand. Graham, watching, was sure now that Niemand had known: the smile and the gesture were for the boy's mental age, not his physical one.

The boy took Niemand's hand. For a moment it seemed that he was going to climb into Niemand's **lap**, and Graham pulled him back gently. He said, 'Go to your room now, Harry.'

The boy **skipped** back into his bedroom, not closing the door.

Niemand's eyes met Graham's and he said, 'I like him,' with obvious **sincerity**. He added, 'I hope that what you're going to read to him will always be true.'

Graham didn't understand. Niemand said, *'Chicken Little,* I mean. It's a fine story—but may *Chicken Little* always be wrong about the sky falling down.'

---

**affection** [ə'fekʃn] Zuneigung, Liebe   **Chicken Little** amer. Märchen: Ein Huhn, von e-r herabfallenden Eichel getroffen, verbreitet Panik mit dem Ruf 'The sky is falling'.   **bashful** ['bæʃful] schüchtern   **lap** [læp] Schoß   **skip** [skɪp] hüpfen   **sincerity** [sɪn'serɪtɪ] Aufrichtigkeit

Graham suddenly had liked Niemand when Niemand had shown liking for the boy. Now he remembered that he must close the interview quickly. He rose, **in dismissal**.

He said, 'I fear you're wasting your time and mine, Mr Niemand. I know all the arguments, everything you can say I've heard a thousand times. Possibly there is truth in what you believe, but it does not **concern** me. I'm a scientist, and only a scientist. Yes, it is public knowledge that I am working on a weapon, a rather **ultimate** one. But, for me personally, that is only a by-product of the fact that I am **advancing** science. I have thought it through, and I have found that that is my only concern.'

'But, Dr Graham, is humanity *ready* for an ultimate weapon?'

Graham **frowned**. 'I have told you my point of view, Mr Niemand.'

Niemand rose slowly from the chair. He said, 'Very well, **if you do not choose** to discuss it, I'll say no more.' He passed a hand across his forehead. 'I'll leave, Dr Graham. I wonder, though … may I change my mind about the drink you offered me?'

Graham's irritation **faded**. He said, 'Certainly. Will whisky and water do?' '**Admirably**.'

Graham excused himself and went into the kitchen. He got the **decanter** of whisky, another of water, ice cubes, glasses.

---

**in dismissal** [dɪsˈmɪsəl] zur Verabschiedung   **concern** [kənˈsɜːn] interessieren, betreffen   **ultimate** [ˈʌltɪmɪt] endgültig   **advance** [ədˈvɑːns] vorwärts bringen   **frown** [fraʊn] die Stirn runzeln   **If you do not choose to …** Wenn Sie lieber nicht … wollen   **fade** [feɪd] schwinden   **admirable** [ˈædmərəbl] großartig   **decanter** [dɪˈkæntə] Karaffe

When he returned to the living room, Niemand was just leaving the boy's bedroom. He heard Niemand's 'Good night, Harry,' and Harry's happy ''Night, Mr Niemand.'

Graham made drinks. A little later, Niemand **declined** a second one and started to leave.

Niemand said, 'I took the liberty of bringing a small **gift** to your son, doctor. I gave it to him while you were getting the drinks for us. I hope you'll forgive me.'

'Of course. Thank you. Good night.'

Graham closed the door; he walked through the living room into Harry's room. He said, 'All right, Harry. Now I'll read to—'

There was sudden sweat on his forehead, but he forced his face and his voice to be calm as he stepped to the side of the bed. 'May I see that, Harry?' When he had it safely, his hands shook as he examined it.

He thought, *only a madman would give a loaded revolver to an idiot.*

8.3.2006

---

**decline** [dɪ'klaɪn] ablehnen     **gift** [gɪft] Geschenk

# The Girls in Their Summer Dresses

*Irwin Shaw*

**Fifth Avenue** was shining in the sun when they left the **Brevoort**. The sun was warm, even though it was February, and everything looked like Sunday morning—the buses and the well-dressed people walking slowly in couples and the quiet buildings with the windows closed.

Michael held **Frances'** arm **tightly** as they walked toward Washington Square in the sunlight. They walked lightly, almost smiling, because they had slept late and had a good breakfast and it was Sunday. Michael unbuttoned his coat and let it flap around him in the mild wind.

'Look out,' Frances said as they crossed Eighth Street. 'You'll break your neck.' Michael laughed and Frances laughed with him.

'She's not so pretty,' Frances said. 'Anyway, not pretty enough to take a chance of breaking your neck.'

Michael laughed again. 'How did you know I was looking at her?'

Frances **cocked her head** to one side and smiled at her husband under the **brim** of her hat. 'Mike, darling,' she said.

'O.K.,' he said. 'Exuse me.'

Frances patted his arm lightly and pulled him along a lit-

---

**Fifth Avenue** ['ævɪnjuː] New Yorker Geschäftsstraße von Weltruf
**Brevoort** [brə'vɔːt] Name e-s Hotels   **Frances** ['frɑːnsɪs] weibl. Vorname   **tight** [taɪt] fest   **cocked her head** ['kɒkt hə 'hed] neigte den Kopf   **brim** [brɪm] Rand, Krempe

tle faster toward Washington Square. 'Let's not see anybody all day,' she said. 'Let's just **hang around** with each other. You and me. We're always up to our neck in people, drinking their Scotch or drinking our Scotch; we only see each other in bed. I want to go out with my husband all day long. I want him to talk only to me and listen only to me.'

'What's **to stop** us?' Michael asked.

'The Stevensons. They want us **to drop by** around one o'-clock and they'll drive us into the country.'

'The **cunning** Stevensons,' Mike said. '**Transparent.** They can **whistle.** They can go driving in the country by themselves.'

'**Is it a date?**'

'It's a date.'

Frances leaned over and kissed him on the tip of the ear.

'Darling,' Michael said, 'this is Fifth Avenue.'

'Let me arrange a program,' Frances said. 'A planned Sunday in New York for a young couple with money to throw away.'

'**Go easy.**'

'First let's go to the Metropolitan Museum of Art,' Frances suggested, because Michael had said during the week he wanted to go.'I haven't been there in three years and there're at least ten pictures I want to see again. Then we can take the bus down to **Radio City** and watch them **skate**. And later we'll go down to **Cavanagh's** and get a steak as big as a **blacksmith's apron**, with a bottle of wine, and after that

---

**hang around** bummeln    **stop** hindern    **drop by** vorbeikommen
**cunning** ['kʌnɪŋ] schlau    **transparent** [træns'peərənt] leicht zu
durchschauen    **whistle** F ['wɪsl] hier: lange darauf warten    **Is it a
date?** Abgemacht?    **Go easy.** Sachte, sachte!    **Radio City** Radio-,
Fernseh- u. Unterhaltungskomplex im sog. Rockefeller Center    **skate**
[skeɪt] Schlittschuh laufen    **Cavanagh's** ['kævənɔːz] Name e-s Speise-
lokals    **blacksmith** ['blæksmɪθ] Hufschmied    **apron** ['eɪprən]
Schürze

there's a French picture at the **Filmarte** that everybody says—say, are you listgening to me?'

'Sure,' he said. He took his eyes off the hatless girl with the dark hair, cut dancer-style like a helmet, who was walking past him.

'That's the program for the day,' Frances said **flatly**. 'Or maybe you'd just rather walk up and down Fifth Avenue.'

'No,' Michael said. 'Not at all.'

'You always look at other women,' Frances said. 'Everywhere. Every damned place we go.'

'No, darling,' Michael said, 'I look at everything. God gave me eyes and I look at women and men in **subway excavations** and **moving pictures** and the little flowers of the field. I **casually** inspect the universe.'

'You ought to see the look in your eye,' Frances said, 'as you casually inspect the universe on Fifth Avenue.'

'I'm a happily married man.' Michael pressed her elbow **tenderly**. 'Example for the whole twentieth century—Mr and Mrs Mike Loomis. Hey, let's have a drink,' he said, stopping.

'We just had breakfast.'

'Now listen, darling,' Mike said, choosing his words with care, 'it's a nice day and we both felt good and there's no reason why we have to break it up. Let's have a nice Sunday.'

'All right. I don't know why I started this. Let's drop it. Let's have a good time.'

The joined hands **consciously** and walked without talking

---

**Filmarte** Name e-s Filmtheaters   **flat** [flæt] matt, stumpf   **subway** AE ['sʌbweɪ] U-Bahn   **excavation** [ekskə'veɪʃn] Schacht   **moving pictures** Pl Kino   **casually** ['kæʒjʊəlɪ] beiläufig, im Vorübergehen   **tender** ['tendə] zärtlich   **conscious** ['kɒnʃəs] bewusst

among the baby carriages and the old Italian men in their Sunday clothes and the young women with **Scotties** in Washington Square Park.

'At least once a year everyone should go to the Metropolitan Museum of Art,' Frances said after a while, her tone a good imitation of the tone she had used at breakfast and at the beginning of their walk. 'And it's nice on Sunday. There're a lot of people looking at the pictures and you get the feeling maybe Art isn't **on the decline** in New York City, after all—'

'I want to tell you something,' Michael said very seriously. 'I have not touched another woman. Not once. In all the five years.'

'All right,' Frances said.

'You believe that, don't you?'

'All right.'

They walked between the crowded benches, under the **scrubby** city-park trees.

'I try not to notice it,' Frances said, 'but I feel **rotten** inside, in my stomach, when we pass a woman and you look at her and I see that look in your eye and that's the way you looked at me the first time. In Alice Maxwell's house. Standing there in the living room, next to the radio, with a green hat on and all those people.'

'I remember the hat,' Michael said.

'The same look,' Frances said. 'And it makes me feel bad. It makes me feel terrible.'

---

**Scotty** F ['skɒtɪ] Scotchterrier    **on the decline** [dɪ'klaɪn] auf dem absteigenden Ast    **scrubby** ['skrʌbɪ] verkümmert    **rotten** sl. ['rɒtn] hundeelend

'Sh-h-h, please, darling, sh-h-h.'

'I think I would like a drink now,' Frances said.

They walked over to a bar on Eighth Street, not saying anything. Michael automatically helping her over **curbstones** and guiding her past automobiles. They sat near a window in the bar and the sun streamed in and there was a small, cheerful fire in the fireplace. A little Japanese waiter came over and put down some **pretzels** and smiled happily at them.

'What do you order after breakfast?' Michael asked.

'Brandy, I suppose,' Frances said.

'Courvoisier,' Michael told the waiter. 'Two Courvoisier.'

The waiter came with the glasses and they sat drinking the brandy in the sunlight. Michael finished half his and drank a little water.

'I look at women,' he said. 'Correct. I don't say it's wrong or right. I look at them. If I pass them on the street and I don't look at them, I'm fooling you, I'm fooling myself.'

'You look at them as though you want them,' Frances said, playing with her brandy glass. 'Every one of them.'

'In a way,' Michael said, speaking softly and not to his wife, 'in a way that's true. I don't do anything about it, but it's true.'

'I know it. That's why I feel bad.'

'Another brandy,' Michael called. 'Waiter, two more brandies.'

He sighed and closed his eyes and rubbed them gently

---

**curbstone** AE = BE kerbstone ['kɜːbstəʊn] Randstein    **pretzel** ['pretsəl] (Salz)Brezel

with his fingertips. 'I love the way women look. One of the things I like best about New York is the battalions of women. When I first came to New York from Ohio that was the first thing I noticed, the million wonderful women, all over the city. I walked around **with my heart in my throat**.'

'A kid,' Frances said. 'That's a kid's feeling.'

'**Guess again**,' Michael said. 'Guess again. I'm older now. I'm a man getting near middle age, putting on a little fat, and I still love to walk along Fifth Avenue at three o'clock on the east side of the street between Fiftieth and the Fifty-seventh Street. They're all out then, shopping, in their **furs** and their crazy hats, everything all concentrated from all over the world into seven **blocks**—the best furs, the best clothes, the **handsomest** women, out to spend money and feeling good about it.'

The Japanese waiter put the two drinks down, smiling with great happiness.

'Everything is all right?' he asked.

'Everything is wonderful,' Michael said.

'If it's just a couple of fur coats,' Frances said, 'and forty-five dollar hats—'

'It's not the fur coats. Or the hats. That's just the scenery for that particular kind of women. Understand,' he said, 'you don't have to listen to this.'

'I want to listen.'

'I like the girls in the offices. **Neat**, with their eyeglasses, smart, **chipper**, **knowing what everything is about**. I like

---

**with my heart in my throat** [hɑːt, θrəʊt] während mir das Herz bis zum Halse schlug    **Guess again** AE [ɡes] Das meinst du!    **fur** [fɜː] Pelz    **block** [blɒk] Häuserblock    **handsome** ['hænsəm] hübsch    **neat** [niːt] adrett, geschmackvoll    **chipper** F ['tʃɪpə] munter, fröhlich    **knowing what everything is about** weltgewandt

the girls on Forty-fourth Street at lunchtime, the actresses, all dressed up **on nothing a week**. I like the salesgirls in the stores, paying attention to you first because you're a man, leaving lady customers waiting. I got all this stuff **accumulated** in me because I've been thinking about it for ten years and now you've asked for it and here it is.'

'Go ahead,' Frances said.

'When I think of New York City, I think of all the girls on parade in the city. I don't know whether it's something special with me or whether every man in the city walks around with the same feeling inside him, but I feel as though I'm at a picnic in this city. I like to sit near the women in the theatres, the famous beauties who've taken six hours to get ready **and look it**. And the young girls at the football games, with the red cheeks, and when the warm weather comes, the girls in their summer dresses.' He finished his drink. 'That's the story.'

Frances finished her drink and **swallowed** two or three times extra. 'You say you love me?'

'I love you.'

'I'm pretty, too,' Frances said. 'As pretty as any of them.'

'You're beautiful,' Michael said.

'I'm good for you,' Frances said, **pleading**. 'I've made a good wife, a good housekeeper, a good friend. I'd do any damn thing for you.'

'I know,' Michael said. He put his hand out and grasped hers.

---

**on nothing a week** für ein paar Cent Wochenlohn   **accumulate** [əˈkjuːmjʊleɪt] aufspeichern   **and look it** und auch danach aussehen   **swallow** [ˈswɒləʊ] schlucken   **pleading** [ˈpliːdɪŋ] flehend, inständig

'You'd like to be free to—' Frances said.

'Sh-h-h.'

'Tell the truth.' She took her hand away from under his.

Michael **flicked** the edge of his glass with his finger. 'O.K.,' he said gently. 'Sometimes I feel I would like to be free.'

'Well,' Frances said, '**any time you say**.'

'Don't be foolish.' Michael swung his chair around to her side of the table and patted her **thigh**.

She began to cry silently into her handkerchief, bent over just enough so that nobody else in the bar would notice. 'Someday,' she said, crying, 'you're going to **make a move**.'

Michael didn't say anything. He sat watching the **bartender** slowly peel a lemon.

'Aren't you?' Frances asked **harshly**. 'Come on, tell me. Talk. Aren't you?'

'Maybe,' Michael said. He moved his chair back again. 'How the hell do I know?'

'You know,' Frances **persisted**. 'Don't you know?'

'Yes,' Michael said after a while, 'I know.'

Frances stopped crying then. Two or three **snuffles** into the handkerchief and she put it away and her face didn't tell anything to anybody. 'At least do me one **favor**,' she said.

'Sure.'

'Stop talking about how pretty this woman is or that one. Nice eyes, nice breasts, a pretty figure, good voice.' She **mimicked** his voice. 'Keep it to yourself. I'm not interested.'

---

**flick** [flɪk] betupfen  **any time you say** jeder Zeit, wenn du willst
**thigh** [θaɪ] Oberschenkel  **make a move** fortgehen  **bartender**
['baːtendə] Barkeeper  **harsh** [haːʃ] schroff  **persist** [pəˈsɪst]
beharren  **snuffle** ['snʌfl] Schluchzer  **favor** AE = BE **favour**
Gefallen  **mimicked** von **mimic** nachahmen

Michael waved to the waiter. 'I'll keep it to myself,' he said.

Frances flicked the corners of her eyes. 'Another brandy,' she told the waiter.

'Two,' Michael said.

'Yes, Ma'am, yes, sir,' said the waiter, backing away.

Frances regarded Michael coolly across the table. 'Do you want me to call the Stevensons?' she asked. 'It'll be nice in the country.'

'Sure,' Michael said. 'Call them.'

She got up from the table and walked across the room toward the telephone. Michael watched her walk, thinking what a pretty girl, what nice legs.

8.3.2006

# The Test

*Angelica Gibbs*

On the afternoon Marian took her second driver's test, Mrs Ericson went with her. 'It's probably better to have someone a little older with you,' Mrs Ericson said as Marian slipped into the driver's seat beside her. 'Perhaps the last time your Cousin Bill made you nervous, talking too much on the way.'

'Yes, Ma'am,' Marian said in her soft unaccented voice. 'They probably do like it better if a white person **shows up** with you.'

'Oh, I don't think it's *that*,' Mrs Ericson began, and **subsided** after a glance at the girl's **set** profile. Marian drove the car slowly through the shady **suburban** streets. It was one of the first hot days in June, and when they reached the boulevard they found it crowded with cars **headed for** the beaches.

'Do you want me to drive?' Mrs Ericson asked. 'I'll be glad to if you're feeling **jumpy**.' Marian shook her head. Mrs Ericson watched her dark, competent hands and wondered for the thousandth time how the house had ever managed to get along without her, or how she had lived through those earlier years when her household had been **presided over** by a series of **slatternly** white girls who had considered housework **demeaning** and the care of children an added insult. 'You drive beautifully, Marian,' she said. 'Now, don't think of

---

**show up** [ʃəʊ] aufkreuzen   **subside** [səbˈsaɪd] hier: verstummen
**set** [set] starr   **suburban** [səˈbɜːbən] Vorstadt-   **headed for** [ˈhedɪd]
unterwegs zu   **jumpy** [ˈdʒʌmpɪ] zappelig   **preside over** [prɪˈzaɪd]
leiten   **slatternly** [ˈslætənlɪ] schlampig   **demeaning** [dɪˈmiːnɪŋ]
erniedrigend

the last time. Anybody would slide on a steep hill on a wet day like that.'

'It takes four mistakes to **flunk** you,' Marian said. 'I don't remember doing all the things the inspector marked down on my **blank**.'

'People say that they only want you to **slip** them a little something,' Mrs Ericson said doubtfully.

'No,' Marian said. 'That would only make it worse, Mrs Ericson, I know.'

The car turned right, at a traffic signal, into a side road and **slid up to the curb** at the rear of a short line of parked cars. The **inspectors** had not arrived yet.

'You have the papers?' Mrs Ericson asked. Marian took them out of her bag: her **learner's permit**, the **car registration**, and her **birth certificate**. They settled down to the **dreary** business of waiting.

'It will be marvellous to have someone **dependable** to drive the children to school every day,' Mrs Ericson said.

Marian looked up from the list of driving **requirements** she had been studying. 'It'll make things simpler at the house, won't it?' she said.

'Oh, Marian,' Mrs Ericson exclaimed, 'if I could only pay you half of what you're worth!'

'Now, Mrs Ericson,' Marian said firmly. They looked at each other and smiled with affection.

Two cars with official **insignia** on their doors stopped across the street. The inspectors leaped out, very **brisk** and

---

**flunk** AE sl. [flʌŋk] durchfallen lassen    **blank** [blæŋk] Formular
**slip** [slɪp] zustecken    **slid up to the curb** AE = BE **kerb** [kɜːb] fuhr
(zum Parken) an den Randstein heran    **inspector** [ɪn'spektə] Prüfer
**learner's permit** ['pɜːmɪt] Lernführerschein (Mindestalter 15 Jahre;
gültig nur in Begleitung e-s Führerscheininhabers u. nur in dem US-
Staat, in dem er ausgestellt wurde)    **car registration** [redʒɪs'treɪʃn]
Kraftfahrzeugschein    **birth certificate** ['bɜːθ sə'tɪfɪkɪt] Geburts-
urkunde    **dreary** ['drɪərɪ] öde    **dependable** [dɪ'pendəbl] zuverlässig
**requirement** [rɪ'kwaɪəmənt] Voraussetzung    **insignia** Pl [ɪn'sɪgnɪə]
Abzeichen Pl    **brisk** [brɪsk] energisch

military in their neat uniforms. Marian's hands **tightened** on the wheel. 'There's the one who flunked me last time,' she whispered, pointing to a **stocky, self-important** man who had begun to shout **directions** at the driver at the head of the line. 'Oh, Mrs Ericson.'

'Now, Marian,' Mrs Ericson said. They smiled at each other again, rather weakly.

The inspector who finally reached their car was not the stocky one but a **genial**, middle-aged man who grinned broadly as he thumbed over their papers. Mrs Ericson started to get out of the car. 'Don't you want to come along?' the inspector asked. '**Mandy** and I don't mind company.'

Mrs Ericson was **bewildered** for a moment. 'No,' she said, and stepped to the curb. 'I might make Marian **self-conscious**. She's a fine driver, Inspector.'

'Sure thing,' the inspector said, **winking** at Mrs Ericson. He slid into the seat beside Marian. 'Turn right at the corner, Mandy-Lou.'

From the curb, Mrs Ericson watched the car move smoothly up the street.

The inspector made notations in a small black book. 'Age?' he inquired **presently**, as they drove along.

'Twenty-seven.'

He looked at Marian out of the corner of his eye. 'Old enough to have quite a **flock of pickaninnies**, eh?'

Marian did not answer.

---

tighten ['taɪtn] fester (zu)fassen   stocky ['stɒkɪ] stämmig
self-important wichtigtuerisch   direction [dɪ'rekʃn] Anweisung
genial ['dʒiːnjəl] freundlich   Mandy(-Lou) ['mændɪ ('luː)] Verball-
hornung von Marian   bewildered [bɪ'wɪldəd] verwirrt
self-conscious ['kɒnʃəs] gehemmt, befangen   wink [wɪŋk] blinzeln
presently ['prezntlɪ] sogleich, bald (darauf)   flock [flɒk] Schar, Horde
pickaninny ['pɪkənɪnɪ] verächtlich: (Neger)Knirps

'Left at this corner,' the inspector said, 'and park between that truck and the green **Buick**.'

The two cars were very close together, but Marian **squeezed** in between them without too much **maneuvering**. 'Driven before, Mandy-Lou?' the inspector asked.

'Yes, sir. I had a **license** for three years in Pennsylvania.'

'Why do you want to drive a car?'

'My employer needs me to take her children to and from school.'

'Sure you don't really want to **sneak out** nights to meet some **young blood**?' the inspector asked. He laughed as Marian shook her head.

'Let's see you take a left at the corner and then turn around in the middle of the next block,' the inspector said. He began to whistle **'Swanee River.'** 'Make you homesick?' he asked.

Marian put out her hand, swung around neatly in the steet, and headed back in the direction from which they had come. 'No,' she said. 'I was born in Scranton, Pennsylvania.'

The inspector **feigned** astonishment. **'You-all ain't** Southern?' he said. 'Well, **dog my cats** if I didn't think you-all came from **down yondah**.'

'No, sir,' Marian said.

'Turn onto Main Street and let's see how you-all does in heavier traffic.'

They followed a line of cars along Main Street for several blocks until they came in sight of a **concrete** bridge which **arched** high **over** the railroad tracks.

---

**Buick** ['bjuɪk] amer. Automarke   **squeeze** [skwi:z] (sich) zwängen **maneuver** AE = BE **manœuvre** [məˈnu:və] manövrieren   **license** AE = BE **licence** ['laɪsəns] hier: Führerschein   **sneak** [sni:k] schleichen **young blood** hier: junger Mann   **'Swanee River'** ['swɒnɪ] Volkslied **feign** [feɪn] heucheln   **you-all ain't** dial. [eɪnt] = **you aren't** (Die mit dial. gekennzeichneten Ausdrücke stammen aus dem Dialekt der Südstaaten der USA.)   **dog my cats** etwa: Hol mich der Henker!   **down yondah** dial. = **down yonder** dort unten   **concrete** ['kɒnkri:t] Beton **arch over** [ɑ:tʃ] sich wölben über

'Read that sign at the end of the bridge,' the inspector said.

'**Proceed with caution. Dangerous in slippery weather**,' Marian said.

'You-all **sho** can read fine,' the inspector exclaimed. 'Where d'you learn to do that, Mandy?'

'I got my college **degree** last year,' Marian said. Her voice was not quite steady.

As the car crept up the **slope** of the bridge the inspector burst out laughing. He laughed so hard he could scarcely give his next direction. 'Stop here,' he said, wiping his eyes, 'then **start 'er** up again. Mandy got her degree, did she? Dog my cats!'

Marian **pulled up** beside the curb. She put the car **in neutral**, pulled on the **emergency**, waited a moment, and then put the car **into gear** again. Her face was set. As she released the brake her foot slipped off the **clutch** pedal and the engine **stalled**.

'Now, **Mistress Mandy**,' the inspector said, 'remember your degree.'

'*Damn* you!' Marian cried. She started the car with a **jerk**.

The inspector lost his joviality in an instant. 'Return to the starting place, please,' he said, and made four very black (30) crosses **at random** in the squares on Marian's **application blank**.

Mrs Ericson was waiting at the curb where they had left her. As Marian stopped the car, the inspector jumped out and

---

**Proceed with caution.** [prə'siːd wɪð 'kɔːʃn] Vorsicht(ig fahren)!
**Dangerous in slippery weather.** ['deɪndʒrəs ɪn 'slɪpərɪ 'weðə] Bei Nässe Schleudergefahr!　**sho** dial. = **sure(ly)**　**degree** [dɪ'griː] akademischer Grad　**slope** [sləʊp] Neigung, Gefälle　**start 'er up.** = **start her up.** Fahren Sie los!　**pull up** [pʊl] anhalten　**put the car in neutral** ['njuːtrəl] in den Leerlauf schalten　**emergency** [ɪ'mɜːdʒənsɪ] Handbremse　**put the car into gear** [gɪə] den Gang einlegen　**clutch** [klʌtʃ] Kupplung　**stall** [stɔːl] absterben, abwürgen　**Mistress Mandy** ['mɪstrɪs] Fräulein Lehrerin M.　**jerk** [dʒɜːk] Ruck　**at random** ['rændəm] wahllos　**application blank** [æplɪ'keɪʃn] Antragsformular, Prüfungsbogen

**brushed past her**, his face purple. 'What happened?' Mrs Ericson asked, and looked after him with alarm.

Marian stared down at the wheel and her lip trembled.

'Oh, Marian, *again*?' Mrs Ericson said.

Marian nodded. 'In a sort of different way,' she said, and slid over to the righthand side of the car.

9.3. 2006

---

**brush past** s.o. an j-m vorbeifegen

# Examination Day

*Henry Slesar*

The Jordans never spoke of the exam, not until their son,
Dickie, was twelve years old. It was on his birthday that Mrs
Jordan first mentioned the subject in his presence, and the
anxious manner of her speech caused her husband to answer
sharply.

'Forget about it,' he said. 'He'll do all right.'

They were at the breakfast table, and the boy looked up
from his plate curiously. He was an **alert-eyed** youngster,
with flat blond hair and a quick, nervous manner. He didn't
understand what the sudden tension was about, but he did
know that today was his birthday, and he wanted harmony
above all. Somewhere in the little apartment there were
wrapped, **beribboned** packages waiting to be opened, and in
the tiny **wall kitchen**, something warm and sweet was being
prepared in the automatic stove. He wanted the day to be
happy, and the **moistness** of his mother's eyes, the **scowl** on
his father's face, spoiled the mood of **fluttering** expectation
with which he had greeted the morning.

'What exam?' he asked.

His mother looked at the tablecloth. 'It's just a sort of Government intelligence test they give children at the age of
twelve. You'll be getting it next week. It's nothing to worry
about.'

---

**alert-eyed** [əˈlɜːtaɪd] mit wachen Augen   **beribboned** [bɪˈrɪbənd] mit
Bändern geschmückt   **wall kitchen** Kochnische   **moistness**
[ˈmɔɪstnɪs] Feuchtigkeit   **scowl** [skaʊl] finsterer Ausdruck   **fluttering**
[ˈflʌtərɪŋ] flatternd, aufgeregt

'You mean a test like in school?'

'Something like that,' his father said, getting up from the table. 'Go read your comic books, Dickie.'

The boy rose and wandered towards that part of the living room which had been 'his' corner since **infancy**. He fingered the topmost comic of the **stack**, but seemed uninterested in the colorful squares of **fast-paced** action. He wandered towards the window, and peered **gloomily** at the **veil** of **mist** that **shrouded** the glass.

'Why did it have to rain *today*?' he said. 'Why couldn't it rain tomorrow?'

His father, now **slumped** into an armchair with the Government newspaper, rattled the sheets in **vexation**. 'Because it just did, that's all. Rain makes the grass grow.'

'Why, Dad?'

'Because it does, that's all.'

Dickie **puckered his brow**. 'What makes it green, though? The grass?'

'Nobody knows,' his father **snapped**, then immediately regretted his abruptness.

Later in the day, it was birthday time again. His mother beamed as she handed over the gaily-colored packages, and even his father **managed** a grin and a **rumple-of-the-hair**. He kissed his mother and shook hands gravely with his father. Then the birthday cake was brought forth, and the ceremonies concluded.

---

**infancy** ['ɪnfənsɪ] frühe Kindheit   **stack** [stæk] Stoß, Stapel   **fast-paced** ['fɑːstpeɪst] schnell ablaufend   **gloomy** ['gluːmɪ] düster, traurig   **veil** [veɪl] Schleier   **mist** [mɪst] Nebel   **shroud** [ʃraʊd] einhüllen   **slumped** [slʌmpt] versunken   **vexation** [vek'seɪʃn] Ärger   **pucker one's brow** [braʊ] die Stirn runzeln   **snap** [snæp] bellen, schnauzen   **managed ... a rumple-of-the-hair** ['rʌmpl] brachte es fertig, (ihm) durch das Haar zu fahren

An hour later, seated by the window, he watched the sun force its way between the clouds.

'Dad,' he said, 'how far away is the sun?'

'Five thousand miles,' his father said.

※

Dick sat at the breakfast table and again saw moisture in his mother's eyes. He didn't connect her tears with the exam until his father suddenly brought the subject to light again.

'Well, Dickie,' he said, with a manly **frown**, 'you've got an appointment today.'

'I know, Dad. I hope—'

'Now it's nothing to worry about. Thousands of children take this test every day. The Government wants to know how smart you are, Dickie. That's all there is to it.'

'I get good marks in school,' he said hesitantly.

'This is different. This is a—special kind of test. They give you this stuff to drink, you see, and then you go into a room where there's a sort of machine—'

'What stuff to drink?' Dickie said.

'It's nothing. It tastes like peppermint. It's just to make sure you answer the questions truthfully. Not that the Government thinks you won't tell the truth, but this stuff makes *sure*.'

Dickie's face showed **puzzlement**, and a **touch** of fright. He looked at his mother, and she composed her face into a misty smile.

---

**frown** [fraʊn] Stirnrunzeln     **puzzlement** [ˈpʌzlmənt] Verwirrung
**touch** [tʌtʃ] Anflug

'Everything will be all right,' she said.

'Of course it will,' his father agreed. 'You're a good boy, Dickie; you'll **make out** fine. Then we'll come home and celebrate. All right?'

'Yes, sir,' Dickie said.

✳

They entered the Government Educational Building fifteen minutes before the appointed hour. They crossed the marble floors of the great **pillared** lobby, passed beneath an **archway** and entered an automatic **elevator** that brought them to the fourth floor.

There was a young man wearing an **insignia-less tunic**, seated at a polished desk in front of Room 404. He held a **clipboard** in his hand, and he checked the list down to the Js and permitted the Jordans to enter.

The room was as cold and official as a courtroom, with long benches flanking metal tables. There were several fathers and sons already there, and a thin-lipped woman with **cropped** black hair was passing out sheets of paper.

Mr Jordan filled out the form, and returned it to the clerk. Then he told Dickie: 'It won't be long now. When they call your name, you just go through the doorway at that end of the room.' He indicated the portal with his finger.

A concealed loudspeaker crackled and called off the first name. Dickie saw a boy leave his father's side **reluctantly** and walk slowly towards the door.

---

**make out** AE F abschneiden (bei e-r Prüfung)   **pillared** ['pɪləd] mit Säulen (versehen)   **archway** ['ɑːtʃweɪ] Torbogen   **elevator** AE ['elɪveɪtə] = **BE lift** Fahrstuhl   **insignia-less tunic** [ɪn'sɪgnɪəlɪs 'tuːnɪk] Uniformrock ohne Rangabzeichen   **clipboard** ['klɪpbɔːd] Klemmbrett   **cropped** [krɒpt] kurz geschoren   **reluctant** [rɪ'lʌktənt] widerwillig

At **five minutes of eleven**, they called the name of Jordan.

'Good luck, son,' his father said, without looking at him. '**I'll call for** you when the test is over.'

Dickie walked to the door and turned the knob. The room inside was **dim**, and he could barely make out the features of the gray-tunicked **attendant** who greeted him.

'Sit down,' the man said softly. He indicated a high stool beside his desk. 'Your name's Richard Jordan?'

'Your classification number is 600–115. Drink this, Richard.'

He lifted a plastic cup from the desk and handed it to the boy. The liquid inside had the consistency of buttermilk, tasted only vaguely of the promised peppermint. Dickie **downed** it, and handed the man the empty cup.

He sat in silence, feeling **drowsy**, while the man wrote busily on a sheet of paper. Then the attendant looked at his watch, and rose to stand only inches from Dickie's face. He **unclipped** a pen-like object from the pocket of his tunic, and flashed a tiny light into the boy's eyes.

'All right,' he said. 'Come with me, Richard.'

He led Dickie to the end of the room, where a single wooden armchair faced a **multi-dialed** computing machine. There was a microphone on the left arm of the chair, and when the boy sat down, he found its **pinpoint** head **conveniently** at his mouth.

'Now just relax, Richard. You'll be asked some questions,

---

five minutes of eleven AE = BE five minutes to eleven    call for
s.o. [kɔːl] j-n abholen    dim [dɪm] trüb, dunkel    attendant
[əˈtendənt] Diensttuender    down F hinunterkippen, -schlucken
drowsy [ˈdraʊzɪ] schläfrig    unclip [ʌnˈklɪp] losklemmen    multi-
dial(l)ed [ˈmʌltɪdaɪəld] mit vielen Messanzeigen    pinpoint
[ˈpɪnpɔɪnt] stecknadelkopfgroß    convenient [kənˈviːnjənt] bequem

and you think them over carefully. Then give your answers into the microphone. The machine will take care of the rest.'

'Yes, sir.'

'I'll leave you alone now. Whenever you want to start, just say 'ready' into the microphone.'

'Yes, sir.'

The man squeezed his shoulder, and left.

Dickie said, 'Ready.'

Lights appeared on the machine, and a mechanism **whirred**. A voice said:

'Complete this sequence. One, four, seven, ten ...'

✳

Mr and Mrs Jordan were in the living room, not speaking, not even **speculating**.

It was almost four o'clock when the telephone rang. The woman tried to reach it first, but her husband was quicker.

'Mr Jordan?'

The voice was **clipped**; a **brisk**, official voice.

'Yes, speaking.'

'This is the Government Educational Service. Your son, Richard M. Jordan, Classification 600–115, has completed the Government examination. We regret to inform you that his intelligence quotient has **exceeded** the Government **regulation**, according to Rule 84, Section 5, of the **New Code**.'

---

**whir(r)** [wɜː] surren  **speculate** [ˈspekjʊleɪt] nachdenken  **clipped** [klɪpt] abgehackt  **brisk** [brɪsk] energisch, bestimmt  **exceed** [ɪkˈsiːd] überschreiten  **regulation** [regjʊˈleɪʃn] Vorschrift  **New Code** [kəʊd] Neue Rechtsordnung

Across the room, the woman cried out, knowing nothing except the emotion she read on her husband's face.

'You may **specify** by telephone,' the voice droned on, 'whether you wish his body **interred** by the Government or would you prefer a private **burial** place? The fee for Government burial is ten dollars.

9.3.2006

---

**specify** ['spesɪfaɪ] angeben   **inter** [ɪn'tɜː] beerdigen   **burial** ['berɪəl] Beisetzung

# The Pedestrian

*Ray Bradbury*

To enter out into that silence that was the city at eight o'-
clock of a **misty** evening in November, to put your feet upon
that **buckling concrete walk**, to step over **grassy seams** and
make your way, hands in pockets, through the silences, that
was what Mr Leonard Mead most dearly loved to do. He
would stand upon the corner of an **intersection** and **peer**
down long moonlit **avenues of sidewalk** in four directions,
deciding which way to go, but it really made no difference;
he was alone in this world of 2053 A.D., or as good as alone,
and with a final decision made, a path selected, he would
stride off, sending patterns of frosty air before him like the
smoke of a cigar.

Sometimes he would walk for hours and miles and return
only at midnight to his house. And on his way he would see
the cottages and homes with their dark windows, and it was
not unequal to walking through a **graveyard** where only the
faintest glimmers of **firefly** light appeared in **flickers** behind
the windows. Sudden gray phantoms seemed to **manifest**
upon inner room walls where a curtain was still undrawn
against the night, or there were whisperings and murmurs
where a window in a **tomb**-like building was still open.

Mr Leonard Mead would pause, **cock** his head, listen,
look, and march on, his feet making no noise on the **lumpy**

---

misty ['mɪstɪ] neblig   **buckling** ['bʌklɪŋ] sich verziehend, sich
wölbend   **concrete walk** ['kɒnkriːt] betonierter Bürgersteig   **grassy
seams** [siːmz] grasbewachsene Fugen   **intersection** [ɪntəˈsekʃn]
Straßenkreuzung   **peer** [pɪə] spähen   **avenues of sidewalk**
['ævɪnjuːz] Prachtpromenaden   **graveyard** ['greɪvjɑːd] Friedhof
**firefly** ['faɪəflaɪ] Leuchtkäfer   **flicker** ['flɪkə] Flimmern   **manifest**
['mænɪfest] erscheinen (Geister)   **tomb** [tuːm] Grab   **cock** [kɒk]
schrägstellen   **lumpy** ['lʌmpɪ] klumpig, aufgesprungen

walk. For long ago he had wisely changed to **sneakers** when strolling at night, because the dogs **in intermittent squads** would **parallel** his journey with barkings if he wore hard heels, and lights might click on and faces appear and an entire street be **startled** by the passing of a lone figure, himself, in the early November evening.

On this particular evening he began his journey in a westerly direction, toward the hidden sea. There was a good crystal frost in the air; it cut the nose and made the lungs **blaze** like a Christmas tree inside; you could feel the cold light going on and off, all the branches filled with invisible snow. He listened to the faint push of his soft shoes through autumn leaves with satisfaction, and whistled a cold quiet whistle between his teeth, occasionally picking up a leaf as he passed, examining its **skeletal pattern** in the infrequent lamplights as he went on, smelling its **rusty** smell.

'Hello, in there,' he whispered to every house on every side as he moved. 'What's up tonight on Channel 4, Channel 7, Channel 9? Where are the cowboys rushing, and do I see the United States Cavalry over the next hill **to the rescue**?'

The street was silent and long and empty, with only his shadow moving like the shadow of a **hawk** in mid-country. If he closed his eyes and stood very still, frozen, he could imagine himself upon the center of a plain, a wintry, windless Arizona desert with no house in a thousand miles, and only dry river beds, the street, for company.

'What is it now?' he asked the houses, noticing his wrist

---

**sneakers** ['sni:kəz] Tuchschuhe   **in intermittent squads** [ɪntə'mɪtənt 'skwɒdz] etwa: wechselweise   **parallel** ['pærəlel] hier: begleiten   **startle** ['stɑːtl] aufschrecken   **blaze** [bleɪz] brennen   **skeletal pattern** ['skelɪtl 'pætən] skelettartiges Muster   **rusty** ['rʌstɪ] rostig   **(coming) to the rescue** ['reskjuː] zu Hilfe (kommend)   **hawk** [hɔːk] Habicht

watch. 'Eight-thirty P.M.? Time for a dozen **assorted** murders? A quiz? A revue? A comedian falling off the stage?'

Was that a murmur of laughter from within a moon-white house? He hesitated, but went on when nothing more happened. He stumbled over a particularly uneven section of sidewalk. The **cement** was **vanishing** under flowers and grass. In ten years of walking by night or day, for thousands of miles, he had never met another person walking, not one in all that time.

He came to a **cloverleaf intersection** which stood silent where two main highways crossed the town. During the day it was a thunderous **surge** of cars, the **gas** stations open, a great insect rustling and a ceaseless **jockeying for position** as the **scarab-beetles**, a faint **incense puttering** from their **exhausts, skimmed** homeward to the far directions. But now these highways, too, were like streams in a dry season, all stone and bed and moon **radiance.**

He turned back on a side street, circling around toward his home. He was within a block of his **destination** when the lone car turned a corner quite suddenly and flashed a **fierce** white **cone** of light upon him. He stood **entranced**, not unlike a night **moth, stunned** by the illumination, and then drawn toward it.

A metallic voice called to him:

'Stand still. Stay where you are! Don't move!'

He halted.

'Put up your hands!'

---

assorted [əˈsɔːtɪd] verschiedenerlei   cement [sɪˈment] Zement
vanish [ˈvænɪʃ] verschwinden   cloverleaf intersection [ˈkləʊvəliːf]
Kleeblattkreuzung   surge [sɜːdʒ] Brandung, Brausen   gas AE [gæs] =
BE petrol [ˈpetrəl] Benzin   jockeying for position [ˈdʒɒkɪŋ] Ein-
fädeln   scarab-beetle [ˈskærəb ˈbiːtl] Skarabäuskäfer   incense
[ˈɪnsens] Weihrauch, hier: Rauchfahne   putter [ˈpʌtə] paffen
exhaust [ɪgˈzɔːst] Auspuff   skim [skɪm] gleiten, kriechen   radiance
[ˈreɪdjəns] strahlender Glanz   destination [destɪˈneɪʃn] Ziel(ort)
fierce [fɪəs] hier: grell   cone [kəʊn] Kegel   entranced [ɪnˈtrɑːnst]
gebannt   moth [mɒθ] Motte, Falter   stunned [stʌnd] wie betäubt

'But—' he said.

'Your hands up! Or we'll shoot!'

The police, of course, but what a rare, incredible thing; in a city of three million, there was only *one* police car left, wasn't that correct? Ever since a year ago, 2052, the election year, the **force** had been cut down from three cars to one. Crime was **ebbing**; there was no need now for the police, **save for** this one lone car wandering and wandering the empty streets.

'Your name?' said the police car in a metallic whisper. He couldn't see the men in it for the bright light in his eyes.

'Leonard Mead,' he said.

'Speak up!'

'Leonard Mead!'

'Business or profession?'

'I guess you'd call me a writer.'

'No profession,' said the police car, as if talking to itself. The light held him fixed, like a museum **specimen**, needle **thrust** through chest.

'You might say that,' said Mr Mead. He hadn't written in years. Magazines and books didn't sell any more. Everything went on in the tomb-like houses at night now, he thought, continuing his **fancy**. The tombs, **ill-lit** by television light, where the people sat like the dead, the gray or multi-colored lights touching their faces, but never really touching them.

'No profession,' said the phonograph voice, **hissing**. 'What are you doing out?'

---

**force** [fɔːs] Stärke, Zahl    **ebb** [eb] verebben, dahinschwinden    **save for** außer    **specimen** ['spesɪmɪn] Exemplar    **thrust** [θrʌst] von **thrust** gestoßen    **fancy** ['fænsɪ] Eingebung    **ill-lit** von **light** schlecht beleuchtet    **hiss** [hɪs] zischen

'Walking,' said Leonard Mead.

'Walking!'

'Just walking,' he said simply, but his face felt cold.

'Walking, just walking, walking?'

'Yes, sir.'

'Walking where? For what?'

'Walking for air. Walking to *see*.'

'Your address!'

'Eleven South Saint James Street.'

'And there is air *in* your house, you have an air *conditioner*, Mr Mead?'

'Yes.'

'And you have a **viewing screen** in your house to see with?'

'No.'

'No?' There was a **crackling quiet** that in itself was an accusation.

'Are you married, Mr Mead?'

'No.'

'Not married,' said the police voice behind the **fiery beam**. The moon was high and clear among the stars and the houses were gray and silent.

'Nobody wanted me,' said Leonard Mead with a smile.

'Don't speak unless you're spoken to!'

Leonard Mead waited in the cold night.

'Just *walking*, Mr Mead?'

'Yes.'

---

**viewing screen** ['vjuːɪŋskriːn] Bildschirm   **crackling quiet** ['kwaɪət] von Prasseln erfüllte Pause   **fiery** ['faɪərɪ] feurig, gleißend   **beam** [biːm] Strahl

'But you haven't exlained for what purpose.'

'I explained; for air, and to see, and just to walk.'

'Have you done this often?'

'Every night for years.'

The police car sat in the center of the street with its **radio throat** faintly **humming**.

'Well, Mr Mead,' it said.

'Is that all?' he asked politely.

'Yes,' said the voice. 'Here.' There was a **sigh**, a **pop**. The back door of the police car sprang wide. 'Get in.'

'Wait a minute, I haven't done anything!'

'Get in.'

'I protest!'

'Mr Mead.'

He walked like a man suddenly drunk. As he passed the front window of the car he looked in. As he had expected, there was no one in the front seat, no one in the car at all.

'Get in.'

He put his hand to the door and peered into the back seat, which was a little cell, a little black jail with **bars**. It smelled of **riveted** steel. It smelled of **harsh** antiseptic; it smelled too clean and hard and metallic. There was nothing soft there.

'Now if you had a wife to give you an alibi,' said the iron voice. 'But—'

'Where are you taking me?'

The car hesitated, or rather gave a faint **whirring** click, as if information, somewhere, was **dropping card by punch-**

---

**radio throat** [θrəʊt] „Lautsprecherrachen"   **hum** [hʌm] summen
**sigh** [saɪ] hier: Knarren   **pop** [pɒp] Knall   **bar** [bɑː] Gitterstab   **rivet**
['rɪvɪt] vernieten   **harsh** [hɑːʃ] hart, scharf   **whir(r)** [wɜː] surren
**drop** [drɒp] tröpfeln lassen, gleiten lassen   **card by punch-slotted
card** Lochkarte um Lochkarte

slotted card under electric eyes. 'To the Psychiatric Center for **Research** on **Regressive** Tendencies.'

He got in. The door shut with a soft **thud**. The police car rolled through the night avenues, flashing its **dim** lights ahead.

They passed one house on one street a moment later, one house in an entire city of houses that were dark, but this one particular house had all of its electric lights brightly lit, every window a loud yellow illumination, square and warm in the cool darkness.

'That's *my* house,' said Leonard Mead.

No one answered him.

The car moved down the empty riverbed streets and off away, leaving the empty streets with the empty sidewalks, and no sound and no motion all the rest of the **chill** November night.

10.3.2006

---

**research** [rɪˈsɜːtʃ] Forschung   **regressive** [rɪˈgresɪv] rückschrittlich, fortschrittsfeindlich   **thud** [θʌd] (dumpfer) Schlag   **dim** [dɪm] trübe, abgeblendet   **chill** [tʃɪl] frostig

# The Chaser

*John Collier*

Alan Austen, as nervous as a kitten, went up certain dark and **creaky** stairs in the neighborhood of **Pell Street**, and **peered** about for a long time on the **dim landing** before he found the name he wanted written **obscurely** on one of the doors.

He pushed open this door, as he had been told to do, and found himself in a tiny room, which contained no furniture but a plain kitchen table, a **rocking-chair**, and an ordinary chair. On one of the dirty **buff-colored** walls were a couple of shelves, containing in all perhaps a dozen bottles and jars.

An old man sat in the rocking-chair, reading a newspaper. Alan, without a word, handed him the card he had been given. 'Sit down, Mr Austen,' said the old man very politely. 'I am glad to make your acquaintance.'

'Is it true,' asked Alan, 'that you have a certain mixture that has—er—quite extraordinary effects?'

'My dear sir,' replied the old man, 'my **stock in trade** is not very large—I don't **deal** in **laxatives** and **teething** mixtures—but such as it is, it is **varied**. I think nothing I sell has effects which could be precisely described as ordinary.'

'Well, the fact is ...' began Alan.

'Here, for example,' interrupted the old man, reaching for a bottle from the shelf. 'Here is a liquid as colourless as water, almost tasteless, quite **imperceptible** in coffee, wine, or any

---

**chaser** ['tʃeɪsə] Schluck zum Nachspülen   **creaky** ['kriːkɪ] knarrend
**Pell Street** Straße im Chinesenviertel von New York   **peer** [pɪə]
spähen   **dim** [dɪm] düster   **landing** ['lændɪŋ] Treppenabsatz
**obscure** [əb'skjʊə] undeutlich   **rocking-chair** ['rɒkɪŋtʃeə] Schaukel-
stuhl   **buff-colo(u)red** [bʌf] lederfarben   **stock in trade**
['stɒkɪn'treɪd] Warenbestand   **deal in** [diːl] handeln mit, führen
**laxative** ['læksətɪv] Abführmittel   **teething** ['tiːðɪŋ] zum Zähne-
bekommen   **varied** ['veərɪd] mannigfaltig   **imperceptible**
[ɪmpə'septəbl] unbemerkbar

*1) z.B. Schnaps auf Kaffee etc.*
*2) Heringsjäger, manchmal voller Weib*

49

other **beverage**. It is also quite impercetible to any known method of **autopsy**.'

'Do you mean it is a poison?' cried Alan, very much horrified.

'Call it a **glove-cleaner** if you like,' said the old man indifferently. 'Maybe it will clean gloves. I have never tried. One might call it a life-cleaner. Lives need cleaning sometimes.'

'I want nothing of that sort,' said Alan.

'Probably it is just as well,' said the old man. 'Do you know the price of this? For one teaspoonful, which is sufficient, I ask five thousand dollars. Never less. Not a penny less.'

'I hope all your mixtures are not as expensive,' said Alan **apprehensively**.

'Oh dear, no,' said the old man. 'It would be no good **charging** that sort of price for a love **potion**, for example. Young people who need a love potion very seldom have five thousand dollars. Otherwise they would not need a love potion.'

'I am glad to hear that,' said Alan.

'I look at it like this,' said the old man. '**Please** a customer with one article, and he will come back when he needs another. Even if it *is* more costly. He will save up for it, if necessary.'

'So,' said Alan, 'you really do sell love potions?'

'If I did not sell love potions,' said the old man, reaching for another bottle, 'I should not have mentioned the other matter to you. It is only when one is in a position to **oblige** that one can afford to be so **confidential**.'

---

beverage ['bevərɪdʒ] Getränk    autopsy ['ɔːtəpsɪ] Autopsie, Leichen-
öffnung    glove-cleaner ['glʌvkliːnə] Reinigungsmittel für Hand-
schuhe    apprehensive [æprɪ'hensɪv] ängstlich    charge [tʃɑːdʒ] verlangen, berechnen    potion ['pəʊʃn] Trank    please [pliːz] zufrieden
stellen    oblige [ə'blaɪdʒ] gefällig sein, dienen    confidential
[kɒnfɪ'denʃl] vertraulich

'And these potions,' said Alan. 'They ar not just—just—er—'

'Oh, no,' said the old man. 'Their effects are permanent, and **extend** far beyond the mere **casual** impulse. But they include it. Oh, yes, they include it. **Bountifully, insistently.** Everlastingly.'

'Dear me!' said Alan, attempting a look of scientific **detachment**. 'How very interesting!'

'But consider the **spiritual** side,' said the old man.

'I do, indeed,' said Alan.

'For indifference,' said the old man, 'they **substitute devotion**. For **scorn, adoration.** Give one tiny measure of this to the young lady—its flavour is imperceptible in orange juice, soup, or cocktails—and however gay and **giddy** she is, she will change altogether. She will want nothing but **solitude** and you.'

'I can hardly believe it,' said Alan. 'She is so fond of parties.'

'She will not like them any more,' said the old man. 'She will be afraid of the pretty girls you may meet.'

'She will **actually** be jealous?' cried Alan in a **rapture**. 'Of me?'

'Yes, she will want to be everything to you.'

'She is, already. Only she doesn't care about it.'

'She will, when she has taken this. She will care intensely. You will be her **sole** interest in life.'

'Wonderful!' cried Alan.

---

extend [ɪks'tend] sich erstrecken, reichen   casual ['kæʒjʊəl] gelegentlich   **bountiful** ['baʊntɪfʊl] (über)reichlich   **insistent** [ɪn'sɪstənt] nachhaltig   detachment [dɪ'tætʃmənt] Distanziertheit   **spiritual** ['spɪrɪtjʊəl] seelisch   **substitute for** ['sʌbstɪtjuːt] an die Stelle setzen von   devotion [dɪ'vəʊʃn] Anhänglichkeit   **scorn** [skɔːn] Verachtung   **adoration** [ædɔː'reɪʃn] Anbetung, Verehrung   **giddy** ['gɪdɪ] hier: leichtsinnig   solitude ['sɒlɪtjuːd] Einsamkeit   **actual** ['æktjʊəl] tatsächlich   rapture ['ræptʃə] Verzückung   sole [səʊl] einzig

'She will want to know all you do,' said the old man. 'All that has happened to you during the day. Every word of it. She will want to know what you are thinking about, why you smile suddenly, why you are looking sad.'

'That is love!' cried Alan.

'Yes,' said the old man. 'How carefully she will look after you! She will never allow you to be tired, to sit in a **draught**, to **neglect** your food. If you are an hour late, she will be terrified. She will think you are killed, or that some **siren** has caught you.'

'I can hardly imagine Diana like that!' cried Alan, **overwhelmed** with joy.

'You will not have to use your imagination,' said the old man. 'And, by the way, since there are always sirens, if by any chance you *should*, later on, **slip** a little, you need not worry. She will forgive you, in the end. She will be terribly hurt, of course, but she will forgive you—in the end.'

'That will not happen,' said Alan **fervently**.

'Of course not,' said the old man. 'But if it did, you need not worry. She would never divorce you. Oh, no! And, of course, she will never give you the least, the very least, grounds for—**uneasiness**.'

'And how much,' said Alan, 'is this wonderful mixture?'

'I is not as **dear**,' said the old man, 'as the glove-cleaner, or life-cleaner, as I sometimes call it. No. That is five thousand dollars, never a penny less. One has to be older than you are, to **indulge in** that sort of thing. One has to save up for it.'

---

**draught** [drɑːft] Zugluft   **neglect** [nɪˈglekt] vernachlässigen
**siren** [ˈsaɪərɪn] Sirene   **overwhelmed** [əʊvəˈwelmd] überwältigt
**slip** [slɪp] e-n Fehltritt begehen   **fervent** [ˈfɜːvənt] leidenschaftlich
**uneasiness** [ʌnˈiːzɪnɪs] Besorgnis   **dear** [dɪə] hier: teuer
**indulge in** [ɪnˈdʌldʒ] frönen

'But the love potion?' said Alan.

'Oh, that,' said the old man, opening the drawer in the kitchen table, and taking out a tiny, rather dirty-looking **phial**. 'That is just a dollar.'

'I can't tell you how grateful I am,' said Alan, watching him fill it.

'I like to oblige,' said the old man. 'Then customers come back, later in life, when they are **better off**, and want more expensive things. Here you are. You will find it very effective.'

'Thank you again,' said Alan. 'Goodbye.'

'**Au revoir**,' said the old man.

*10. 3. 2006*

---

**phial** ['faɪəl] Fläschchen    **better off** vermögender    **Au revoir** franz. [o rə'vwaːr] Auf Wiedersehen

# The Unicorn in the Garden

*James Thurber*

Once upon a sunny morning a man who sat in a breakfast **nook** looked up from his scrambled eggs to see a white unicorn with a gold horn quietly **cropping** the roses in the garden. The man went up to the bedroom where his wife was asleep and woke her. 'There's a unicorn in the garden,' he said. 'Eating roses.'

She opened one unfriendly eye and looked at him. 'The unicorn is a **mythical beast**,' she said, and turned her back on him.

The man walked slowly downstairs and out into the garden. The unicorn was still there; he was now **browsing** among the **tulips**. 'Here, unicorn,' said the man, and he pulled up a **lily** and gave it to him. The unicorn ate it gravely.

With a high heart, because there was a unicorn in his garden, the man went upstairs and **roused** his wife again. 'The unicorn,' he said, 'ate a lily.'

His wife sat up in bed and looked at him, coldly. 'You are a **booby**,' she said, 'and I am going to have you put in the **booby-hatch**.'

The man, who had never liked the words *booby* and *booby-hatch* and who liked them even less on a shining morning when there was a unicorn in the garden, thought for a moment. 'We'll see about that,' he said. He walked over to the

---

**unicorn** [ˈjuːnɪkɔːn] Einhorn   **nook** [nʊk] Ecke, Nische   **crop** [krɒp] abfressen   **mythical beast** [ˈmɪθɪkəl ˈbiːst] Fabeltier   **browse** [braʊz] weiden   **tulip** [ˈtjuːlɪp] Tulpe   **lily** [ˈlɪlɪ] Lilie   **rouse** [raʊz] wachrütteln   **booby** [ˈbuːbɪ] Dummkopf   **booby-hatch** AE F [ˈbuːbɪhætʃ] „Klapsmühle"

door. 'He has a golden horn in the middle of his forehead,' he told her. Then he went back to the garden to watch the unicorn; but the unicorn had gone away. The man sat down among the roses and went to sleep.

As soon as the husband had gone out of the house, the wife got up and dressed as fast as she could. She was very excited and there was a **gloat** in her eye. She telephoned the police and she telephoned a psychiatrist; she told them to hurry to her house and bring a **strait-jacket**.

When the police and the psychiatrist arrived they sat down in chairs and looked at her, with great interest.

'My husband,' she said, 'saw a unicorn this morning.'

The police looked at the psychiatrist and the psychiatrist looked at the police.

'He told me it ate a lily,' she said.

The psychiatrist looked at the police and the police looked at the psychiatrist.

'He told me it had a golden horn in the middle of its forehead,' she said.

At a **solemn** signal from the psychiatrist, the police leaped from their chair and seized the wife. They had a hard time **subduing** her, for she put up a terrific struggle, but they finally subdued her. Just as they got her into the strait-jacket, the husband came back into the house.

'Did you tell your wife you saw a unicorn?' asked the police.

'Of course not,' said the husband. 'The unicorn is a myth-

---

**gloat** [gləʊt] Schadenfreude    **strait-jacket** ['streɪtdʒækɪt] Zwangs-jacke    **solemn** ['sɒləm] feierlich, ernst    **subdue** [sʌb'djuː] überwältigen

ical beast.' 'That's all I wanted to know,' said the psychiatrist. 'Take her away. I'm sorry, sir, but your wife is as **crazy as a jay bird**.' So they took her away, cursing and screaming, and shut her up in an **institution**. The husband lived happily ever after.

*Moral:* **Don't count your boobies until they are hatched.**

10.3.2006

---

**as crazy as a jay bird** total verrückt    **institution** [ɪnstɪ'tjuːʃn]
Anstalt    **Don't count your boobies ...** scherzhafte Abwandlung von
**Don't count your chickens until they are hatched ...** bevor sie aus-
geschlüpft sind

# News of the Engagement

*Arnold Bennett*

I wrote to my mother regularly every week, telling her most of my doings. She knew all my friends by name. I dare say she formed in her mind **notions** of what sort of people they were. Thus I had frequently mentioned Agnes and her family in my letters. But you can't write even to your mother and say in cold blood:'I think I am beginning to fall in love with Agnes,' 'I think Agnes likes me', 'I am mad on her,' 'I feel certain she likes me,' 'I shall **propose to** her on such a day.' You can't do that. At least I couldn't. **Hence** it had come about that on the 20th of December I had proposed to Agnes and been accepted by Agnes, and my mother had no **suspicion** that my happiness was so near. And on the 22nd, by a **previous** and **unalterable** arrangement, I had come to spend Christmas with my mother.

I was the only son of a widow; I was all that my mother had. And **lo**! I had gone and engaged myself to a girl she had never seen, and I had kept her in the dark! She would certainly be extremely surprised, and she might be a little bit hurt—just at first. Anyhow, the situation was **the least in the world** delicate.

I walked up the whitened front steps of my mother's little house, just opposite where the electric cars stop, but before I could put my hand on the bell my little **plump** mother, in

---

**engagement** [ɪnˈgeɪdʒmənt] Verlobung    **notion** [ˈnəʊʃn] Vorstellung
**propose to** [prəˈpəʊz] e-n Heiratsantrag machen    **hence** [hens] folglich    **suspicion** [səˈspɪʃn] Verdacht, Ahnung    **previous** [ˈpriːvjəs]
vorherig    **unalterable** [ʌnˈɔːltərəbl] unabänderlich    **lo** [ləʊ] siehe!
**the least in the world** ein klein bisschen    **plump** [plʌmp] mollig

her black silk and her gold **brooch** and her **auburn** hair, opened to me, having doubtless watched me down the road from the **bay**-window, as usual, and she said, as usual, kissing me.

'Well, Philip! How are you?'

And I said.

'Oh! I'm all right, mother. How are you?'

I perceived instantly that she was more excited than my arrival ordinarily made her. There were tears in her smiling eyes, and she was as nervous as a young girl. She did indeed look remarkably young for a woman of forty-five, with twenty-five years of widowhood and a **brief** but too **tempestuous** married life behind her.

The thought flashed across my mind: 'By some means or other she has got wind of my engagement. But how?'

But I said nothing. I, too, was naturally rather nervous. Mothers are **kittle cattle**.

'I'll tell her at supper,' I decided.

And she **hovered** round me, like a **sea-gull** round a steamer, as I went upstairs.

There was a ring at the door. She flew, instead of letting the servant go. It was a porter with my bag.

Just as I was coming downstairs again there was another ring at the door. And my mother appeared magically out of the kitchen, but I was beforehand with her, and with a laugh I insisted on opening the front door myself this time. A young woman stood on the step.

---

**brooch** [brəʊtʃ] Brosche    **auburn** ['ɔːbən] kastanienbraun    **bay** [beɪ] Erker    **brief** [briːf] kurz    **tempestuous** [tem'pestjʊəs] stürmisch    **kittle cattle** unberechenbar    **hover** ['hɒvə] schweben    **sea-gull** ['siːgʌl] Möwe

'Please, Mrs Dawson wants to know if Mrs Durance can kindly lend her half-a-dozen knives and forks?'

'Eh, with pleasure,' said my mother, behind me. 'Just wait a minute, Lucy. Come inside on the mat.'

I followed my mother into the drawing-room, where she kept her silver in a **cabinet**.

'That's Mrs Dawson's new servant,' my mother whispered. 'But she needn't think I'm going to lend her my best, because I'm not.'

'I shouldn't if I were you,' I supported her.

And she went out with some secondbest in **tissue paper**, and **beamed** on Mrs Dawson's servant with an **assumed benevolence**.

'There!' she exclaimed. 'And **the compliments of the season** to your mistress, Lucy.'

After that my mother disappeared into the kitchen to **worry** an entirely capable servant. And I roamed about, feeling happily excited, examining the drawing-room, in which nothing was changed except the **incandescent** light and the picture postcards on the mantelpiece. Then I wandered into the dining-room, a small room at the back of the house, and here an immense surprise awaited me.

Supper was set for three!

'Well,' I reflected. 'Here's a nice state of affairs! Supper for three, and she hasn't **breathed a word**!'

My mother was so clever in social matters, and especially in the planning of delicious surprises, that I believed her ca-

---

**cabinet** ['kæbɪnɪt] Schränkchen   **tissue paper** ['tɪsjuː] Seidenpapier
**beam** [biːm] strahlen   **assumed** [ə'sjuːmd] vorgetäuscht
**benevolence** [bɪ'nevələns] Wohlwollen   **the compliments of the season** ['kɒmplɪmənt, 'siːzn] die besten Wünsche zum Fest   **worry** ['wʌrɪ] plagen   **incandescent** [ɪnkæn'desnt] Glüh-, elektrisch   **not to breathe a word** [briːð] kein Sterbenswörtchen sagen

pable even of miracles. In some way or other she must have discovered the state of my desires towards Agnes. She had written, or something. She and Agnes had been **plotting** together by letter to **startle** me, and perhaps telegraphing. Agnes had **fibbed** in telling me that she could not possibly come to **Bursley** for Christmas; she had delightfully fibbed. And my mother had got her **concealed** somewhere in the house, or was **momentarily** expecting her. That explained the tears, the nervousness, the rushes to the door.

I crept out of the dining-room, determined not to let my mother know that I had secretly **viewed** the supper-table. And as I was crossing the lobby to the drawing-room there was a third ring at the door, and a third time my mother rushed out of the kitchen.

'By Jove!' I thought. 'Suppose it's Agnes. What a scene!'

And trembling with expectation I opened the door.

It was Mr Nixon.

Now, Mr Nixon was an old friend of the family's, a man of forty-nine or fifty, with a **reputation** for **shrewdness** and increasing wealth. He owned a hundred and seventy-five cottages in the town, having bought them gradually in half-dozens, and in rows, he collected the rents himself, and **attended to** the repairs himself, and was **celebrated** as a good **landlord**, and as being almost the only man in Bursley who had **made cottage property pay**. He lived alone in Commerce Street, and, though not **talkative**, was usually jolly, with one or two good stories **tucked away** in the cor-

---

**plot** [plɒt] ein Komplott schmieden    **startle** ['stɑːtl] überraschen
**fib** [fɪb] flunkern    **Bursley** ['bɜːzlɪ] Stadt in Mittelengland (eigentlicher Name: **Burslem**)    **conceal** [kən'siːl] verstecken    **momentarily** ['məʊməntərɪlɪ] jeden Augenblick    **view** [vjuː] in Augenschein nehmen    **reputation** [repju(ː)'teɪʃn] Ruf    **shrewdness** ['ʃruːdnɪs] Schlauheit    **attend to** [ə'tend] erledigen    **celebrated** ['selɪbreɪtɪd] berühmt    **landlord** ['lænlɔːd] Hauseigentümer, Vermieter    **make cottage property pay** ['kɒtɪdʒ 'prɒpətɪ] mit Hausbesitz Gewinne erzielen    **talkative** ['tɔːkətɪv] gesprächig    **tucked away** [tʌkt] verstaut, versteckt

ners of his memory. He was my mother's **trustee**, and had morally aided her in the **troublous** times before my father's early death.

'Well, young man,' cried he. 'So you're back in **owd Bosley**!' It amused him to speak the dialect a little occasionally.

And he brought his **burly**, powerful form into the lobby.

I greeted him as **jovially** as I could, and then he shook hands with my mother, neither of them speaking.

'Mr Nixon is come for supper, Philip,' said my mother.

I liked Mr Nixon, but I was not too well pleased by this information, for I wanted to talk **confidentially** to my mother. I had a task before me with my mother, and here Mr Nixon was **plunging into the supper**. I could not **break it gently to** my mother that I was engaged to a strange young woman in the presence of Mr Nixon. Mr Nixon had been in to supper several times during previous visits of mine, but never on the first night.

However, I had to make the best of it. And we sat down and began on the ham, the sausages, the eggs, the **crumpets**, the toast, the jams, the **mince-tarts**, the Stilton, and the **celery**. But we none of us ate very much, despite my little plump mother's protestations.

My suspicion was that perhaps something had gone slightly wrong with my mother's affairs, and that Mr Nixon was taking the first opportunity to explain things to me. But such a possibility did not interest me, for I could easily afford

---

**trustee** [trʌs'tiː] Vermögensverwalter    **troublous** ['trʌbləs] veraltet: unruhig    **owd Bosley** [əʊd] = old Bursley    **burly** ['bɜːlɪ] stämmig    **jovial** ['dʒəʊvɪəl] heiter    **confidentially** [kɒnfɪ'denʃlɪ] im Vertrauen, vertraulich    **plunge into the supper** [plʌndʒ] zum Abendessen hereinplatzen    **break it gently to s.o.** es j-m schonend beibringen    **crumpet** ['krʌmpɪt] Teekuchen    **mince-tart** ['mɪnstɑt] Pastete    **Stilton** ['stɪltn] engl. Rahmkäse    **celery** ['selərɪ] Sellerie

61

to keep my mother and a wife too. I was still **preoccupied in** my engagement—and surely there is nothing astonishing in that—and I began to compose the words in which, immediately on the departure of Mr Nixon after supper, I would **tackle my mother on the subject**.

When we had reached the Stilton and celery, I **intimated** that I must walk down to the post-office, as I had to **dispatch** a letter.

'Won't it do tomorrow, my **pet**?' asked my mother.

'It will not,' I said.

Imagine leaving Agnes two days without news of my safe arrival and without assurances of my love! I had started writing the letter in the train, near Willesden, and I finished it in the drawing-room.

'A lady in the case?' Mr Nixon called out gaily.

'Yes,' I replied with firmness.

I went forth, bought a picture postcard showing St. Luke's Square, Bursley, most untruthfully picturesque, and posted the card and the letter to my darling Agnes. I hoped that Mr Nixon would have departed **ere** my return; he had made no **reference** at all during supper to my mother's affairs. But he had not departed. I found him **solitary** in the drawing-room, smoking a very fine cigar.

'Where's the **mater**?' I demanded.

'She's just gone out of the room,' he said. 'Come and sit down. Have a **weed**. I want a bit of a chat with you, Philip.'

---

**preoccupied in** [pri(ɪ)'ɒkjʊpaɪd] vertieft in, erfüllt von    **tackle s.o. on the subject** j-m die Sache eröffnen    **intimate** ['ɪntɪmeɪt] zu verstehen geben    **dispatch** [dɪs'pætʃ] aufgeben, absenden    **pet** [pet] Liebling    **ere** [eə] poet. vor    **reference** ['refrəns] Hinweis, Anspielung    **solitary** ['sɒlɪtərɪ] einsam, allein    **mater** sl. ['meɪtə] Mutter    **weed** sl. [wiːd] Zigarre, „Kraut"

I obeyed, taking one of the very fine cigars.

'Well, Uncle Nixon,' I encouraged him, wishing to get the chat over because my mind was full of Agnes. I sometimes called him uncle for fun.

'Well, my boy,' he began. 'It's no use **me beating about the bush**. What do you think of me as a **stepfather**?'

I was **struck**, as they say down there, **all of a heap**.

'What?' I stammered. 'You don't mean to say—you and mother—?'

He nodded.

'Yes, I do, **lad**. Yesterday she promised she'd marry my unworthy self. It's been coming along for some time. But I don't expect she's given you any **hint** in her letters. In fact, I know she hasn't. It would have been rather difficult, wouldn't it? She couldn't well have written, 'My dear Philip, an old friend, Mr Nixon, is falling in love with me and I believe I'm falling in love with him. One of these days he'll be proposing to me.' She couldn't have written like that, could she?'

I laughed. I could not help it.

'Shake hands,' I said warmly. 'I'm delighted.'

And soon afterwards my mother **sidled in**, shyly.

'The lad's delighted, Sarah,' said Mr Nixon shortly.

I said nothing about my own engagement that night. I had never thought of my mother as a woman with a future. I had never realized that she was desirable, and that a man might desire her, and that her lonely existence in that house

---

**beat about the bush** [bʊʃ] um die Sache herumreden    **stepfather** ['stepfɑːðə] Stiefvater    **struck all of a heap** sprachlos    **lad** [læd] Junge    **hint** [hɪnt] Wink, Andeutung    **sidle in** ['saɪdl] hereinschleichen

was not all that she had the right to demand from life. And I was ashamed of my characteristic **filial** selfish egoism. So I decided that I would not **intrude** my joy on hers until the next morning. **We live and learn**.

10.3.3006

---

**filial** ['fɪljəl] kindlich    **intrude** [ɪn'truːd] aufzwingen    **We live and learn.** Man lernt nie aus.

# Dr Abraham

*William Somerset Maugham*

A man I had known at St. Thomas's Hospital was a Jew named Abraham, a blond, rather stout young man, shy and very **unassuming**; but he had remarkable gifts. He entered the hospital with a **scholarship**, and during the five years of the **curriculum** gained every prize that was open to him. He was made **house-physician** and **house-surgeon**. His brilliance was allowed by all. Finally he was elected to a position on the **staff**, and his career was assured. So far as human things can be predicted, it was certain that he would rise to the greatest heights of his profession. Honours and wealth awaited him. Before he entered upon his new duties he wished to take a holiday, and, having no private means, he went as surgeon on a **tramp steamer** to the **Levant**. It did not generally carry a doctor, but one of the senior surgeons at the hospital knew a director of the line, and Abraham was taken as a favour.

In a few weeks the **authorities** received his **resignation** of the **coveted** position on the staff. It created **profound** astonishment, and wild rumours were **current**. Whenever a man does anything unexpected, his fellows **ascribe** it to the most **discreditable** motives. But there was a man ready to step into Abraham's shoes, and Abraham was forgotten. Nothing more was heard of him. He vanished.

---

**unassuming** [ˌʌnəˈsjuːmɪŋ] anspruchslos, bescheiden   **scholarship** [ˈskɒləʃɪp] Stipendium   **curriculum** [kəˈrɪkjʊləm] Studienplan **house-physician** [fɪˈzɪʃən] Assistenzarzt (, der im Krankenhaus wohnt)   **house-surgeon** [ˈsɜːdʒən] Chirurg (, der im Krankenhaus wohnt)   **staff** [staːf] Personal, (Ärzte)Kollegium   **tramp steamer** [ˈtræmpstiːmə] Trampschiff   **Levant** [lɪˈvænt] Levante, Länder am östlichen Mittelmeer   **authorities** [ɔːˈθɒrɪtɪz] Behörde   **resignation** [rezɪɡˈneɪʃn] Rücktritt, Verzicht   **covet** [ˈkʌvɪt] begehren   **profound** [prəˈfaʊnd] tief   **current** [ˈkʌrənt] im Umlauf   **ascribe** [əsˈkraɪb] zuschreiben   **discreditable** [dɪsˈkredɪtəbl] ehrenrührig

It was perhaps ten years later that one morning on board
ship, about to land at **Alexandria**, I was **bidden** to line up
with the other passengers for the doctor's examination. The
doctor was a stout man in shabby clothes, and when he took
off his hat I noticed that he was very **bald**. I had an idea that
I had seen him before. Suddenly I remembered.

'Abraham,' I said.

He turned to me with a **puzzled** look, and then, recogniz-
ing me, seized my hand. After expressions of surprise on ei-
ther side, hearing that I meant to spend the night in Alexandria, he asked me to dine with him at the English Club.
When we met again I declared my astonishment at finding
him there. It was a very **modest** position that he occupied,
and there was about him an **air of straitened circumstance**.
Then he told me his story.

When he set out on his holiday in the **Mediterranean** he
had every intention of returning to London and his **appointment** at St. Thomas's. One morning the tramp docked
at Alexandria, and from the deck he looked at the city, white
in the sunlight, and the crowd on the **wharf**; he saw the na-
tives in their shabby **gabardines**, the blacks from the Sudan,
the noisy **throng** of Greeks and Italians, the grave Turks in
**tarbooshes**, the sunshine and the blue sky; and something
happened to him. He could not describe it. It was like a thun-
der-clap, he said, and then, dissatisfied with this, he said it
was like a **revelation**. Something seemed to twist his heart,
and suddenly he felt an **exultation**, a sense of wonderful

---

**Alexandria** [ælɪg'zɑːndrɪə] Hafenstadt in Ägypten    **bidden** von **bid**
aufgefordert    **bald** [bɔːld] kahl(-köpfig)    **puzzled** ['pʌzld] verdutzt
**modest** ['mɒdɪst] bescheiden    **air of straitened circumstance**
['streɪtnd 'sɜːkəmstəns] Aussehen e-s Mannes, der in beschränkten
Verhältnissen lebt    **Mediterranean** [medɪtə'reɪnjən] Mittelmeer
**appointment** [ə'pɔɪntmənt] Ernennung, Amt    **wharf** [wɔːf] Kai
**gabardine** ['gæbədiːn] hier: Kittel    **throng** [θrɒŋ] Gedränge
**tarboosh** [tɑːr'buːʃ] Fes    **revelation** [revɪ'leɪʃn] Offenbarung
**exultation** [egzʌl'teɪʃn] Jubel

freedom. He felt himself at home, and he made up his mind there and then, in a minute, that he would live the rest of his life in Alexandria. He had no great difficulty in leaving the ship, and in twenty-four hours, with all his belongings, he was on shore.

'The Captain must have thought you **as mad as a hatter**,' I smiled.

'I didn't care what anybody thought. It wasn't I that acted, but something stronger within me. I thought I would go to a little Greek hotel, while I looked about, and I felt I knew where to find one. And do you know, I walked straight there, and when I saw it I recognized it at once.'

'Had you been to Alexandria before?'

'No; I'd never been out of England in my life.'

**Presently** he entered the Government service, and there he had been ever since.

'Have you never regretted it?'

'Never, not for a minute. I earn just enough to live upon, and I'm satisfied. I ask nothing more than to remain as I am till I die. I've had a wonderful life.'

I left Alexandria next day, and I forgot about Abraham till a little while ago, when I was dining with another old friend in the profession, Alec Carmichael, who was in England on short **leave**. I ran across him in the street and congratulated him on the **knighthood** with which his eminent services during the war had been rewarded. We arranged to spend an evening together **for old time's sake**, and when I agreed to

---

**as mad as a hatter** ['hætə] total übergeschnappt    **presently** ['prezntlı] sogleich, bald danach    **leave** [liːv] Urlaub    **knighthood** ['naɪthʊd] (Erhebung in den) Adelsstand    **for old time's sake** zur Erinnerung an alte Zeiten

dine with him, he proposed that he should ask nobody else, so that we could chat without interruption. He had a beautiful old house in Queen Anne Street, and being a man of taste he had furnished it admirably. When his wife, a tall, lovely creature in cloth of gold, had left us, I remarked laughingly on the change in his present circumstances from those when we had both been medical students. We had looked upon it then as an extravagance to dine in a shabby Italian restaurant in the Westminster Bridge Road. Now Alec Carmichael was on the staff of half a dozen hospitals. I should think he earned ten thousand a year, and his knighthood was but the first of the honours which must **inevitably fall to his lot.**

'I've done pretty well,' he said, 'but the strange thing is that I owe it all to one piece of luck.'

'What do you mean by that?'

'Well, do you remember Abraham? He was the man who had the future. When we were students he **beat me all along the line.** He got the prices and the scholarships that I went in for. I always played second fiddle to him. If he'd kept on he'd be in the position I'm in now. That man had a genius for surgery. Poor devil, he's gone to the dogs altogether. He's got some **twopenny-halfpenny** job in the **medical** at Alexandria—**sanitary officer** or something like that. I'm told he lives with an ugly old Greek woman and has half a dozen **scrofulous** kids. The fact is, I suppose, that it's not enough to have brains. The thing that counts is character. Abraham hadn't got character.'

---

**inevitable** [ɪnˈevɪtəbl] zwangsläufig    **fall to s.o.'s lot** j-m zufallen
**beat s.o. all along the line** j-n auf der ganzen Linie schlagen
**twopenny-halfpenny job** [ˈtʌpnɪˈheɪpnɪ] Arbeit für einen Hunger-
lohn    **medical (= medical service)** Gesundheitswesen    **sanitary
officer** [ˈsænɪtərɪ ˈɒfɪsə] Beamter im Gesundheitswesen    **scrofulous**
[ˈskrɒfjʊləs] skrofulös, hautkrank

Character? I should have thought it needed a good deal of character to throw up a career after half an hour's meditation, because you saw in another way of living a more intense **significance**. And it required still more character never to regret the sudden step. But I said nothing, and Alec Carmichael **proceeded reflectively**:

'Of course it would be **hypocritical** for me to pretend that I regret what Abraham did. After all, I've **scored** by it.' He puffed luxuriously at the long Corona he was smoking. 'But if I weren't personally **concerned** I should be **sorry at the waste**. It seems a **rotten thing** that a man should **make such a hash of life**.'

I wondered if Abraham really had made a hash of life. Is to do what you most want, to live under the conditions that please you, in peace with yourself, to make a hash of life; and is it success to be an eminent surgeon with ten thousand a year and a beautiful wife? I suppose it depends on what meaning you attach to life, the **claim** which you **acknowledge** to society, and the claim of the individual. But again I held my tongue, for who am I to argue with a knight?

9.3.2006

---

significance [sɪgˈnɪfɪkəns] Bedeutung    proceed [prəˈsiːd] fortfahren
**reflective** [rɪˈflektɪv] nachdenklich    **hypocritical** [hɪpəˈkrɪtɪkl]
heuchlerisch    **score** [skɔː] profitieren    **concerned** [kənˈsɜːnd]
betroffen    **be sorry at the waste** [weɪst] bedauern, dass j-d s-e Fähig-
keiten so verkommen lässt    **rotten thing** sl. [ˈrɒtn] Schweinerei
**make a hash of s.th.** et. verpfuschen    **claim** [kleɪm] Anspruch,
Anrecht    **acknowledge** [əkˈnɒlɪdʒ] zugestehen

# The Snob

*Morley Callaghan*

It was at the **book counter** in the **department store** that
John Harcourt, the student, **caught a glimpse** of his father.
At first he could not be sure in the crowd that pushed along
the **aisle**, but there was something about the color of the
back of the elderly man's neck, something about the **faded**
felt hat, that he knew very well. Harcourt was standing with
the girl he loved, buying a book for her. All afternoon he had
been talking to her, eagerly, but with an anxious **diffidence**,
as if there still remained in him an **innocent** wonder that she
should be delighted to be with him. From underneath her
**wide-brimmed** straw hat, her face, so fair and beautifully
strong with its expression of cool independence, kept turning up to him and sometimes smiled at what he said. That
was the way they always talked, never daring to show much
full, strong feeling. Harcourt had just bought the book, and
had reached into his pocket for the money with a free, **ready
gesture** to make it appear that he was accustomed to buying
books for young ladies, when the white-haired man in the
faded felt hat, at the other end of the counter, turned half-to-
ward him, and Harcourt knew he was standing only a few
feet away from his father.

The young man's easy words **trailed away** and his voice
became little more than a whisper, as if he were afraid that

---

**book counter** ['kaʊntə] Bücherstand    **department store** [dɪ'pɑ:tmənt
stɔ:] Kauf-, Warenhaus    **catch a glimpse of** [glɪmps] (j-n) flüchtig
erblicken    **aisle** [aɪl] Gang (zwischen den Tischen)    **faded** ['feɪdɪd]
verblichen, verschossen    **diffidence** ['dɪfɪdəns] Schüchternheit
**innocent** ['ɪnəsnt] unschuldig, kindlich    **wide-brimmed**
['waɪdbrɪmd] breitrandig    **ready** ['redɪ] bereitwillig, rasch    **gesture**
['dʒestʃə] Geste, Bewegung    **trail away** [treɪl] sich verlieren

everyone in the store might recognize it. There was rising in him a **dreadful uneasiness**; something very precious that he wanted to hold seemed close to destruction. His father, standing at the end of the **bargain** counter, was planted **squarely** on his two feet, turning a book over thoughtfully in his hands. Then he took out his glasses from an old, worn leather case and adjusted them on the end of his nose, looking down over them at the book. His coat was thrown open; two buttons on his vest were **undone**, his hair was too long, and in his rather shabby clothes he looked very much like a workingman, a **carpenter** perhaps. Such a **resentment** rose in young Harcourt that he wanted to cry out bitterly, 'Why does he dress as if he never owned a decent suit in his life? He doesn't care what the whole world thinks of him. He never did. I've told him a hundred times he ought to wear his good clothes when he goes out. Mother's told him the same thing. He just laughs. And now Grace may see him. Grace will meet him.'

So young Harcourt stood still, with his head down, feeling that something very painful was **impending**. Once he looked anxiously at Grace, who had turned to the bargain counter. Among those people **drifting aimlessly** by with hot red faces, getting in each other's way, using their elbows but keeping their faces **detached** and wooden, she looked tall and splendidly alone. She was so sure of herself, her relation to the people in the aisles, the clerks behind the counters, the books on the shelves, and everything around her. Still keep-

---

**dreadful** ['dredfʊl] furchtbar    **uneasiness** [ʌn'iːzɪnɪs] Unbehagen
**bargain** ['baːgɪn] hier: Gelegenheitskauf    **squarely** ['skweəlɪ] vierschrötig    **undone** ['ʌn'dʌn] von **undo** ['ʌn'duː] aufgeknüpft, offen
**carpenter** ['kaːpɪntə] Zimmermann    **resentment** [rɪ'zentmənt] Groll,
Unmut    **impend** [ɪm'pend] bevorstehen, drohen    **drift** [drɪft] (sich)
treiben (lassen)    **aimless** ['eɪmlɪs] ziellos    **detached** [dɪ'tætʃt]
gleichgültig, distanziert

ing his head down and moving close, he whispered uneasily, 'Let's go and have tea somewhere, Grace.'

'In a minute, dear,' she said.

'Let's go now.'

'In just a minute, dear,' she repeated absently.

'There's not a breath of air in here. Let's go now.'

'What makes you so impatient?'

'There's nothing but old books on that counter.'

'There may be something here I've wanted all my life,' she said, smiling at him brightly and not noticing the uneasiness in his face.

So Harcourt had to move slowly behind her, getting closer to his father all the time. He could feel the space that separated them narrowing. Once he looked up with a vague, **sidelong glance**. But his father, red-faced and happy, was still reading the book, only now there was a **meditative** expression on his face, as if something in the book had **stirred** him and he intended to stay there reading for some time.

Old Harcourt had lots of time to amuse himself, because he was on a pension after working hard all his life. He had sent John to the university and he was eager to have him **distinguish** himself. Every night when John came home, whether it was early or late, he used to go into his father and mother's bedroom and turn on the light and talk to them about the interesting things that had happened to him during the day. They listened and shared this new world with him. They both sat up in their night clothes, and, while his mother asked all

---

**sidelong glance** ['saɪdlɒŋ 'glɑːns] Seitenblick   **meditative** ['medɪtətɪv] nachdenklich   **stir** [stɜː] bewegen, neugierig machen **distinguish o.s.** [dɪs'tɪŋgwɪʃ] sich auszeichnen

the questions, his father listened attentively with his head **cocked** on one side and a smile or a **frown** on his face. The memory of all this was in John now, and there was also a **desperate longing** and a pain within him growing harder to bear as he glanced fearfully at his father, but he thought **stubbornly**, 'I can't introduce him. It'll be easier for everybody if he doesn't see us. I'm not ashamed. But it will be easier. It'll be more **sensible**. It'll only **embarrass** him to see Grace.' By this time he knew he was ashamed, but he felt that his shame was **justified**, for Grace's father had the smooth, **confident** manner of a man who had lived all his life among people who were rich and sure of themselves. Often when he had been in Grace's home talking politely to her mother, John had kept on thinking of the **plainness** of his own home and of his parents' laughing, **good-natured untidiness**, and he resolved desperately that he must make Grace's people admire him.

He looked up **cautiously**, for they were about eight feet away from his father, but at that moment his father, too, looked up and John's glance **shifted swiftly** far over the aisle, over the counters, seeing nothing. As his father's blue, calm eyes stared steadily over the glasses, there was an instant when their glances might have met. Neither one could have been certain, yet John, as he turned away and began to talk hurriedly to Grace, knew surely that his father had seen him. He knew it by the steady calmness in his father's blue eyes. John's shame grew, and then **humiliation sickened** him as he waited and did nothing.

---

cocked [kɒkt] geneigt    frown [fraʊn] Stirnrunzeln, finsterer Ausdruck    desperate ['despərɪt] verzweifelt    longing ['lɒŋɪŋ] Verlangen    stubborn ['stʌbən] eigensinnig    sensible ['sensɪbl] vernünftig    embarrass [ɪm'bærəs] in Verlegenheit bringen    justified ['dʒʌstɪfaɪd] gerechtfertigt    confident ['kɒnfɪdənt] selbstsicher    plainness ['pleɪnnɪs] Schlichtheit    good-natured ['gʊd'neɪtʃəd] gutmütig, gemütlich    untidiness [ʌn'taɪdɪnɪs] Unordentlichkeit    cautious ['kɔːʃəs] vorsichtig    shift [ʃɪft] wechseln, sich verlagern    swift [swɪft] rasch    humiliation [hjʊmɪlɪ'eɪʃn] Demütigung, Erniedrigung    sicken ['sɪkn] anwidern

His father turned away, going down the aisle, walking **erectly** in his shabby clothes, his shoulders very straight, never once looking back. His father would walk slowly down the street, he knew, with that meditative expression deepening and becoming grave.

Young Harcourt stood beside Grace, brushing against her soft shoulder, and **made faintly aware** again of the delicate **scent** she used. There, so close beside him, she was holding within her everything he wanted to reach out for, only he felt a sharp **hostility** that made him **sullen** and silent.

'You were right, John,' she was **drawling** in her soft voice. 'It does get unbearable in here on a hot day. Do let's go now. Have you ever noticed that department stores after a time can make you really hate people?' But she smiled when she spoke, so he might see that she really hated no one.

'You don't like people, do you?' he said sharply.

'People? What people? What do you mean?'

'I mean,' he went on **irritably**, 'you don't like the kind of people you bump into here, for example.'

'Not especially. Who does? What are you talking about?

'Anybody could see you don't,' he said **recklessly**, full of a **savage** eagerness to hurt her. 'I say you don't like simple, honest people, the kind of people you meet all over the city.' He **blurted** the words **out** as if he wanted to shake her, but he was **longing to say**, 'You wouldn't like my family. Why couldn't I take you home to have dinner with them? You'd turn up your nose at them, because they've no **pretensions**.

---

erect [ɪ'rekt] aufrecht    **... made faintly aware** ... undeutlich gewahr werdend    **scent** [sent] Parfum    **hostility** [hɒs'tɪlɪtɪ] Feindseligkeit    **sullen** ['sʌlən] mürrisch    **drawl** [drɔːl] gedehnt sprechen    **irritable** ['ɪrɪtəbl] gereizt    **reckless** ['reklɪs] rücksichtslos    **savage** ['sævɪdʒ] wild, grausam    **blurt out** [blɜːt] hervorstoßen    **he was longing to say** es trieb ihn zu sagen    **pretension** [prɪ'tenʃn] Dünkel

As soon as my father saw you, he knew you wouldn't want to meet him. I could tell by the way he turned.'

His father was on his way home now, he knew, and that evening at dinner they would meet. His mother and sister would talk rapidly, but his father would say nothing to him, or to anyone. There would only be Harcourt's memory of the **level** look in the blue eyes, and the knowledge of his father's pain as he walked away.

Grace watched John's **gloomy** face as they walked through the store, and she knew he was **nursing** some private rage, and so her own resentment and **exasperation** kept growing, and she said, **crisply**, 'You're **entitled to** your **moods** on a hot afternoon, I suppose, but if I feel I don't like it here, then I don't like it. You wanted to go yourself. Who likes to spend very much time in a department store on a hot afternoon? I begin to hate every stupid person that **bangs into** me, everybody near me. What does that make me?'

'It makes you a snob.'

'So I'm a snob now?' she asked angrily.

'Certainly you're a snob,' he said. They were at the door going out to the street. As they walked in the sunlight, in the crowd moving slowly down the street, he was **groping** for words to describe the secret thoughts he had always had about her. 'I've always known how you'd feel about people I like who didn't fit into your private world,' he said.

---

level ['levl] hier: ruhig, verständig   gloomy ['glu:mɪ] finster   **nurse** [nɜːs] hegen, nähren   exasperation [ɪgzɑːspə'reɪʃn] Erbitterung   crisp [krɪsp] scharf, entschieden   **entitled to** [ɪn'taɪtld] berechtigt zu   mood [muːd] Stimmung, Laune   **bang into s.o.** j-n anrempeln   grope [grəʊp] tasten, suchen

'You're a very stupid person,' she said. Her face was **flushed** now, and it was hard for her to express her **indignation,** so she stared straight ahead as she walked along.

They had never talked in this way, and now they were both quickly eager to hurt each other. With a flow of words, she started to **argue** with him, then she **checked herself** and said calmly, 'Listen, John, I imagine you're tired of my company. There's no sense in having tea together. I think I'd better leave you right here.'

'That's fine,' he said. 'Good afternoon.'

'Goodbye.'

'Goodbye.'

She started to go, she had gone two **paces,** but he reached out desperately and held her arm, and he was frightened, and **pleading,** 'Please don't go, Grace.'

All the anger and irritation had left him; there was just a desperate anxiety in his voice as he pleaded, 'Please forgive me. I've no right to talk to you like that. I don't know why I'm so **rude** or what's the matter. I'm **ridiculous.** I'm very, very ridiculous. Please, you must forgive me. Don't leave me.'

He had never talked to her so brokenly, and his **sincerity,** the depth of his feeling, began to stir her. While she listened, feeling all the **yearning** in him, they seemed to have been brought closer together, by opposing each other, than ever before, and she began to feel almost shy. 'I don't know what's the matter. I suppose we're both irritable. It must be the weather,' she said. 'But I'm not angry, John.'

---

**flushed** [flʌʃt] gerötet   **indignation** [ɪndɪgˈneɪʃn] Empörung   **argue** [ˈɑːgjuː] streiten   **check o.s.** [tʃek] innehalten   **pace** [peɪs] Schritt   **plead** [pliːd] flehen   **rude** [ruːd] grob, heftig   **ridiculous** [rɪˈdɪkjʊləs] lächerlich   **sincerity** [sɪnˈserɪtɪ] Aufrichtigkeit   **yearning** [ˈjɜːnɪŋ] Sehnsucht

He nodded his head miserably. He longed to tell her that he was sure she would have been charming to his father, but he had never felt so **wretched** in his life. He held her arm tight, as if he must hold it, or what he wanted most in the world would slip away from him, yet he kept thinking, as he would ever think, of his father walking away quietly with his head never turning.

10. 3. 2000

---

**wretched** ['retʃɪd] elend

# Inexperience

*Frank Tuohy*

The girl stood with her back to the bar, slightly in everyone's way. A pretty girl, she was wearing a dress with a **flared skirt** that she wore at cocktail parties. She swung her foot **to and fro**, and looked around her at the dull groups of raincoated men, whom she took to be **commercial travellers**. Her **glances** always ended with a little gesture of **irritation**, as if these people and these places were too boring and typical; then she took up her glass, **pretending** to drink deeply. She usually **sipped** a very little, sometimes nothing at all. She let the beer touch her mouth and slide back into the glass. She wanted to make it last a long time.

The young man had on a **patched** tweed coat and **service dress** trousers; he was about twenty-two and had just come out of the Army. He was looking down at the top of the bar. Neither of them spoke.

Now another young man pushed his way towards the bar, where, after exchanging a few words with the landlord, he **peered** round about him until he saw the couple. Their expressions and their way of standing were arranged for the general public, not for each other. He could guess that they had not been talking.

'Hullo, hullo!' the newcomer said. He was tall and had a **fair handsome** face; his expensive overcoat hung open.

---

**flared skirt** [fleəd] Glockenrock    **to and fro** [frəʊ] hin und her
**commercial traveller** [kə'mɜːʃl] Handelsvertreter    **glance** [glɑːns]
Blick    **irritation** [ɪrɪ'teɪʃn] Ärger    **pretend** [prɪ'tend] vortäuschen, so
tun als ob    **sip** [sɪp] nippen    **patched** [pætʃt] geflickt    **service dress**
Uniform    **peer** [pɪə] spähen, blicken    **fair** [feə] hell    **handsome**
['hænsəm] hübsch

'Oh, Colin. You know Colin, don't you?'

'Of course I know Colin.' The girl turned her face, bright with her **anxiety** to be liked, full on him.

'Hullo there, Fred.' Colin called girls 'Fred', but he seemed **embarrassed**. 'Have I kept you waiting?'

'Waiting?' the girl asked, **puzzled**, for she had not expected to see him at all. She looked at her young man, but he did not help her.

'I'm sorry,' Colin said suddenly, **rousing** himself. 'What are you drinking?'

'Oh, thank you,' the girl said, 'but I'm all right with this one.' The young man was **frowning at** Colin across her head.

'I see.' He **caught the landlord's eye**, and bought drinks for himself and his friend. 'What've you been doing?'

'We went to the **Curzon**,' the girl said helpfully. 'It was really awfully good, wasn't it, Andrew?'

'You said you liked it,' her young man answered.

'Well, you liked it too, you know you did.'

'Me?' **He made an incredulous voice**. 'I thought it **stank**.'

'Then why did you take me to it, if you thought it was so awful?' she asked **crossly**.

To interrupt, Colin said: 'What was this film, Fred? You haven't said what it was yet.'

She told him the name of the film. 'Have you seen it?'

'Yes.'

'Well, you liked it, surely?'

---

**anxiety** [æŋ'zaɪətɪ] Bestreben   **embarrassed** [ɪm'bærəst] verlegen
**puzzled** ['pʌzld] verdutzt   **rouse o.s.** [raʊz] sich aufraffen,
zusammennehmen   **frown at** [fraʊn] stirnrunzelnd betrachten
... **caught the landlord's eye** machte den Wirt auf sich aufmerksam
**Curzon** ['kɜːzn] Name eines Kinos   **he made an incredulous voice**
[ɪn'kredjʊləs] er ließ seine Stimme ungläubig klingen   **stank** von
**stink** war hundsmiserabel   **cross** [krɒs] ärgerlich, böse

Colin looked across at Andrew, laughing. 'I must say I thought it stank, too.'

The girl made a curious **trapped** movement of her head. 'It was **jolly good**,' she said, **blinking**. 'I thought it was jolly good.' She examined the **stitching** of one of her gloves and started humming a little **tune** to herself; then she came back at Andrew **savagely**: 'It's your turn to buy a drink.'

He made a hopeless face at her. 'Tisha, you know perfectly well I haven't any more money. I told you.'

Colour **flooded into** her cheeks. She had forgotten, and she was **genuinely** sorry, for she did not want to be unkind to him. Earlier, at the beginning of the whole thing, she had firmly decided not to mind about his being poor.

'Give me a cigarette then,' she said quite softly. 'Look, there's a table free, why don't we sit down?'

But she felt their resistance as she said it, and again she had the feeling that she had said the wrong thing. They remained standing, and soon afterwards the two men began a conversation about people she didn't know. Without listening to them she smoked her cigarette in little **puffs**, with a slight frown.

'Tom and Maria,' Colin was saying. 'They're in a pretty bad **way**. I've been up there all afternoon and I did say we'd go back there. I don't think they should be left alone.'

The girl looked from one to the other, her eyes half-closed, as if trying in a **sophisticated** way to **sum them up**.

'What sort of thing was happening?'

---

**trapped** [træpt] ertappt, genarrt    **jolly good** ['dʒɒlɪ] prima    **blink** [blɪŋk] zwinkern    **stitching** ['stɪtʃɪŋ] Naht    **tune** [tjuːn] Melodie    **savage** ['sævɪdʒ] wild, wütend    **flood into** [flʌd] schießen in    **genuine** ['dʒenjʊɪn] echt, wirklich    **puff** [pʌf] Zug (beim Rauchen)    **way** [weɪ] hier: Lage    **sophisticated** [səˈfɪstɪkeɪtɪd] weltklug, „überlegen"    **sum up** einschätzen

'The usual things. They'll probably be turned out of the **studio**.'

'I see.'

The girl watched Andrew carefully whenever he talked. She was anxious about him. It had been Sunday afternoon and she was aware that all had not gone very well. She had **dressed up**, but he had appeared in his oldest clothes. He had not spoken much; it became **increasingly obvious** to her that he reserved his humour for **state occasions**. One always realized things so much more deeply after the cinema: coming out of the Curzon this afternoon into the cold streets of early summer, she knew that he no longer tried to interest her. **Without meaning to**, she sighed; but neither of them noticed.

Colin said rather loudly: 'Yes, I told them I'd go back and bring you.'

She looked up at him. She hadn't known they were going to meet Colin this evening, and there was something not right about his being there. **Nevertheless**, his presence might make the evening easier.

'We must do that, then,' Andrew said. He turned to the girl and began explaining carefully and unnaturally. 'Tom and Maria—these friends of ours— you've heard me speak of them? Well, Tom's wife's been writing to him again and they're both very depressed.'

'I see.'

---

**studio** ['stjuːdɪəʊ] Atelierwohnung   **dress up** sich hübsch anziehen
**increasingly obvious** [ɪnˈkriːsɪŋlɪ ˈɒbvɪəs] immer klarer   **state occasion** ['steɪt əˈkeɪʃn] besondere Gelegenheit   **without meaning to** ohne es zu wollen, unwillkürlich   **nevertheless** [nevəðəˈles] nichtsdestoweniger

'Colin's been out there this afternoon—he only came back again to see us. He said we'd go up there tonight.'

'Of course, why not?' Since this **fitted in with** her idea of being among other people this evening, she let herself agree with what he was saying. 'Well, let's go there then.'

'But, Tisha, it'll be a great **bore**.' His voice was quieter.

'I don't see why, they're friends of yours, aren't they?'

'But, Tisha—'

'When do we start?'

'Not you, Tisha.'

The suddenness of the **hurt** made her **gasp** and lose all balance for a moment; her expression became **ragged** and **wild-looking**. She had known, perhaps long ago, that they were arriving at this point. It was too soon, though, far too soon.

'Well—I—really!'

'But, Tisha,' he was going on saying, 'you don't know these people.'

'I know I don't. But am I so awful that I can't be shown to them? You'd think I was a **pariah** or something. Look, I want to meet your friends. I know you don't think I want to, but I do.' Suddenly it was important for her to fight, though she hated herself for it.

'Try not **to get into a flap**. Colin has only just told me I have to go and see these people. I don't want to go, it's a long way and it'll probably be very dull.'

'Where ist it?'

---

**fit in with** übereinstimmen mit   **bore** [bɔː] langweilige Angelegenheit   **hurt** [hɜːt] Kränkung   **gasp** [gɑːsp] schwer atmen   **ragged** ['rægɪd] rauh, brüchig   **wild-looking** [waɪld] verstört   **pariah** ['pærɪə] Paria, Ausgestoßener   **get into a flap** [flæp] F sich aufregen

'Hampstead.'

'Hampstead's not very far.'

'Well, beyond Hampstead then. Anyway, we're not going to have a gay time, a smart time. It wouldn't be at all interesting for you.'

'How do you know?' she asked him. 'You think just because I don't belong to your **lot** and I still live at home, that I don't know anything at all.'

'It isn't that—'

'If you mean they won't like me, why don't you say so? Is there something I've done wrong?'

'No, really, Tisha, stop this.' He gave a **groan** of tiredness. '**Why do you always put everything on to yourself?**'

'Because I believe that's what it's all about. I don't think you're going anywhere. I think you're just trying to get rid of me.'

'Tisha, you heard Colin tell me, didn't you? You heard him say that Tom and Maria wanted to see me?'

She gave a little hard laugh, but she could not quite turn and call the other young man a liar. 'It all sounds very **suspicious** to me,' she said. 'Why don't you let him go by himself?' She **jerked** her head **rudely** at Colin, who was looking at himself in the mirror-glass behind the shelves of the bar. He turned, but his glance seemed to slide away from her face.

'They asked me to go too,' Andrew said. 'I can't **let them down.**'

'What about me? You had a **previous** appointment to take

---

Hampstead ['hæmstɪd] Stadtteil im NW Londons   **lot** [lɒt] Gruppe
**groan** [grəʊn] Stöhnen   **Why do you always put everything on to yourself?** Warum beziehst du immer alles auf dich?   **suspicious** [sə'spɪʃəs] verdächtig   **jerk** [dʒɜːk] hier: nicken (mit)   **rude** [ruːd] heftig   **let down** im Stich lassen   **previous** ['priːvjəs] vorherig

me out.' An idea came to her. 'I want to go out with you. Look, if it's because you haven't any money, I'll go home and borrow some from my brother.'

There was a silence while Andrew finished his drink. She watched him furiously, **twisting** her gloves in her hands. He put his glass down and said: 'I didn't want to tell you this, Tisha. Tom tried to **commit suicide** last week.'

This **stunned** her—for a moment he thought it was because she took it as a huge lie. Then he saw that she believed him.

'Oh, I see.' Her voice came thin and **strained**. 'Well, I don't see what you can do about it. He's not going to do it again, is he? He probably only did it to **show off**.'

'How dare you say a thing like that?'

'No, I'm sorry—I—'

'What right have you to **suggest** such things—you, just a **spoiled** little girl who talks too much.'

She looked at him and for a moment she was horrified with herself. She was sure now that she would not see him again, but she knew she would go on loving him for some time yet.

'We ought to go,' Colin said, looking at his watch.

'I don't know where I'm going to go,' she said **pathetically**, 'all dressed up like this. I've said I'll be out to dinner. Please couldn't you take me with you—I'll wait outside.'

Andrew, avoiding going near her, almost shouted: 'I tell you, Tisha, it's not possible.'

---

**twist** [twɪst] drehen   **commit suicide** [kə'mɪt 'sjuːsaɪd] Selbstmord begehen   **stun** [stʌn] betäuben, niederschmettern   **strained** [streɪnd] gezwungen, unnatürlich   **show off** angeben   **suggest** [sə'dʒest] andeuten   **spoiled** [spɔɪld] verwöhnt   **pathetic** [pə'θetɪk] trübselig, kläglich

Their eyes met, wounded, angry and **meaningless**. They stared at each other for some time.

'Oh, very well, then. Good night.'

She went towards the door, her head held up, **tottering** a little on black **court shoes** with too-high heels. They watched her until she had gone.

Andrew **broke into** a **sniggering mockdance**.

'Oh God! Damn, damn, damn! More drink, quickly. You know, you saved me, being there. I thought I was going to **give in**.'

'Let's go out somewhere and get drunk, shall we?'

'Yes—**look out**!'

She was standing between them, her face white and shocked.

'I've left one of my gloves behind,' she said.

11. 3. 2006

---

**meaningless** ['miːnɪŋlɪs] ausdruckslos    **totter** ['tɒtə] wanken    **court shoes** [kɔːt] Pumps    **broke into a sniggering mock-dance** ['snɪɡərɪŋ 'mɒkdɑːns] kicherte und vollführte eine Art Freudentanz
**give in** nachgeben    **look out** aufpassen

# Eveline

*James Joyce*

She sat at the window watching the evening **invade** the **avenue**. Her head was leaned against the window curtains, and in her **nostrils** was the odour of dusty **cretonne**. She was tired.

Few people passed. The man out of the last house passed on his way home; she heard his footsteps clacking along the **concrete** pavement and afterwards **crunching** on the **cinder** path before the new red houses. One time there used to be a field there in which they used to play every evening with other people's children. Then a man from Belfast bought the field and built houses in it—not like their little brown houses, but bright brick houses with shining roofs. The children of the avenue used to play together in that field—the **Devines**, the Water, the Dunns, little **Keogh** the cripple, she and her brothers and sisters. Ernest, however, never played: he was too grown up. Her father used often to **hunt them in** out of the field with his **blackthorn** stick; but usually little Keogh used **to keep *nix*** and call out when he saw her father coming. Still they seemed to have been rather happy then. Her father was not so bad then; and besides, her mother was alive. That was a long time ago; she and her brothers and sisters were all grown up; her mother was dead. Tizzie Dunn was dead, too, and the Waters had gone back to England.

---

**invade** [ɪnˈveɪd] hier: sich ausbreiten über   **avenue** [ˈævɪnjuː] Allee, Hauptstraße   **nostrils** [ˈnɒstrɪlz] Nase(nlöcher)   **cretonne** [kreˈtɒn] Kretonne (Baumwollgewebe)   **concrete** [ˈkɒnkriːt] Beton   **crunch** [krʌntʃ] knirschen   **cinder** [ˈsɪndə] Schlacke   **Devine** [dəˈvaɪn], **Keogh** [kjəʊ] Familiennamen   **hunt ... in** nach Hause jagen **blackthorn** [ˈblækθɔːn] Schlehdorn   **keep nix** sl. Schmiere stehen

Everything changes. Now she was going to go away like the others, to leave her home.

Home! She looked round the room, **reviewing** all its **familiar** objects which she had dusted once a week for so many years, wondering where on earth all the dust came from. Perhaps she would never see again those familiar objects from which she had never dreamed of being divided. And yet during all those years she had never found out the name of the priest whose yellowing photograph hung on the wall above the broken harmonium beside the coloured print of the **promises** made to **Blessed Margaret Mary Alacoque**. He had been a school friend of her father. Whenever he showed the photograph to a visitor her father used to pass it with a **casual** word:

'He is in Melbourne now.'

She had **consented** to go away, to leave her home. Was that wise? She tried to weigh each side of the question. In her home anyway she had **shelter** and food; she had those whom she had known all her life about her. Of course she had to work hard, both in the house and at business. What would they say of her in the **Stores** when they found out that she had run away with a fellow? Say she was a fool, perhaps; and her place would be filled up by **advertisement**. Miss Gavan would be glad. She had always **had an edge on her**, especially whenever there were people listening.

'Miss Hill, don't you see these ladies are waiting?'

'**Look lively**, Miss Hill, please.'

---

**review** [rɪ'vjuː] überprüfen   **familiar** [fə'mɪljə] vertraut   **promises** ['prɒmɪsɪz] hier: Verheißungen   **blessed** ['blesɪd] gesegnet, heilig **Margaret Mary Alacoque** franz. Nonne (1647–1690)   **casual** ['kæʒjʊəl] beiläufig   **consent** [kən'sent] einwilligen   **shelter** ['ʃeltə] Obdach   **stores** Pl [stɔːz] Kaufhaus   **advertisement** [əd'vɜːtɪsmənt] Inserat, Annonce   **have an edge on s.o.** [edʒ] j-n von oben herab behandeln   **look lively** ['laɪvlɪ] Tempo!

She would not cry many tears at leaving the Stores.

But in her new home, in a distant unknown country, it would not be like that. Then she would be married—she, Eveline. People would treat her with respect then. She would not be treated as her mother had been. Even now, though she was over nineteen, she sometimes felt herself in danger of her father's **violence**. She knew it was that that had given her the **palpitations**. When they were growing up he had never **gone for** her, like he used to go for Harry and Ernest, because she was a girl; but **latterly** he had begun to threaten her and say what he would do to her **only for her dead mother's sake**. And now she had nobody to protect her. Ernest was dead and Harry, who was in the church decorating business, was nearly always down somewhere in the country. Besides, the **invariable squabble** for money on Saturday nights had begun to weary her unspeakably. She always gave her entire wages—seven shillings—and Harry always sent up what he could, but the trouble was to get any money from her father. He said she used to **squander** the money, that she had no head, that he wasn't going to give her his hard-earned money to throw about the streets, and much more, for he was usually **fairly** bad on Saturday night. In the end he would give her the money and ask her had she any intention of buying Sunday's dinner. Then she had to rush out as quickly as she could and do her **marketing**, holding her black leather purse **tightly** in her hand as she elbowed her way through the crowds and returning home late

---

**violence** ['vaɪələns] Gewalttätigkeit    **palpitation** [pælpɪ'teɪʃn] Herzklopfen    **go for** losgehen auf    **latterly** ['lætəlɪ] neuerdings    **only for her dead mother's sake** wenn er sich nicht um ihrer toten Mutter willen zurückhalten würde    **invariable** [ɪn'veərɪəbl] ständig **squabble** ['skwɒbl] Zank    **squander** ['skwɒndə] vergeuden    **fairly** ['feəlɪ] ziemlich    **marketing** ['mɑːkɪtɪŋ] Einkäufe auf dem Markt **tight** [taɪt] fest

under her load of **provisions**. She had hard work to keep the house together and to see that the two young children who had been left to her **charge** went to school regularly and got their meals regularly. It was hard work—a hard life—but now that she was about to leave it she did not find it a wholly **undesirable** life.

She was about to **explore** another life with Frank. Frank was very kind, manly, open-hearted. She was to go away with him by the night-boat to be his wife and to live with him in Buenos Ayres, where he had a home waiting for her. How well she remembered the first time she had seen him; he was lodging in a house on the main road where she used to visit. It seemed a few weeks ago. He was standing at the gate, his **peaked cap** pushed back on his head and his hair **tumbled** forward over a face of bronze. Then they had come to know each other. He used to meet her outside the Stores every evening and **see her home**. He took her to see *The Bohemian Girl* and she felt **elated** as she sat in an unaccustomed part of the theatre with him. He was awfully fond of music and sang a little. People knew that they were **courting** and, when he sang about the **lass** that loves a sailor, she always felt pleasantly confused. He used to call her Poppens out of fun. First of all it had been an excitement for her to have a fellow and then she had begun to like him. He had tales of distant countries. He had started as a deck boy at a pound a month on a ship of the Allan Line going out to Canada. He told her the names of the ships he had been on

---

**provisions** [prə'vɪʒənz] Nahrungsmittel    **charge** [tʃɑːdʒ] Obhut
**undesirable** ['ʌndɪ'zaɪərəbl] nicht wünschenswert, unerfreulich
**explore** [ɪks'plɔː] hier: kennen lernen    **peaked cap** [piːkt] Schirm-
mütze    **tumble** ['tʌmbl] fallen    **see s.o. home** j-n heimbegleiten
**The Bohemian Girl** [bəʊ'hiːmjən] „Das Mädchen aus Böhmen" (Oper
aus dem Jahre 1843)    **elated** [ɪ'leɪtɪd] freudig erregt    **court** [kɔːt]
den Hof machen, „miteinander gehen"    **lass** [læs] Mädchen

and the names of the different services. He had sailed through the **Straits of Magellan** and he told her stories of the terrible **Patagonians**. He had **fallen on his feet** in Buenos Ayres, he said, and had come over to the old country just for a holiday. Of course, her father had found out the affair and had forbidden her to have anything to say to him.

'I know these sailor chaps,' he said.

One day he had quarelled with Frank, and after that she had to meet her lover scretly.

The evening deepened in the avenue. The white of two letters in her **lap** grew **indistinct**. One was to Harry; the other was to her father. Ernest had been her favourite, but she liked Harry too. Her father was becoming old lately, she noticed; he would miss her. Sometimes he could be very nice. Not long before, when she had been **laid up** for a day, he had read her out a ghost story and made toast for her at the fire. Another day, when their mother was alive, they had all gone for a picnic to the Hill of **Howth**. She remembered her father putting on her mother's **bonnet** to make the children laugh.

Her time was running out, but she continued to sit by the window, leaning her head against the window curtain, **inhaling** the odour of dusty cretonne. Down far in the avenue she could hear a **street organ** playing. She knew the **air**. Strange that it should come that very night to remind her of the promise to her mother, her promise to keep the home together as long as she could. She remembered the last night of her mother's illness; she was again in the **close**, dark room at

---

**Straits of Magellan** ['streɪts əv mə'gelən] Magellanstraße (an der Südspitze Südamerikas)    **Patagonians** [pætə'gəʊnjənz] Indianer in Patagonien    **fall on one's feet** „auf die Füße fallen", Erfolg haben    **lap** [læp] Schoß    **indistinct** [ɪndɪs'tɪŋkt] undeutlich, verschwommen    **laid up** bettlägerig    **Howth** [həʊθ] Ort in der Bucht von Dublin    **bonnet** ['bɒnɪt] Haube    **inhale** [ɪn'heɪl] tief einatmen    **street organ** ['striːt 'ɔːgən] Leierkasten    **air** [eə] Melodie    **close** [kləʊs] schwül, dumpf

the other side of the hall and outside she heard a melancholy air of Italy. The organ-player had been ordered to go away and given sixpence. She remembered her father **strutting** back into the sickroom saying:

'Damned Italians! coming over here!'

As she **mused** the **pitiful** vision of her mother's life **laid its spell on the very quick of her being**—that life of **commonplace sacrifices** closing in final craziness. She trembled as she heard again her mother's voice saying constantly with foolish **insistence**:

'**Derevaun Seraun**! Derevaun Seraun!'

She stood up in a sudden impulse of terror. Escape! She must ecape! Frank would save her. He would give her life, perhaps love, too. But she wanted to live. Why should she be unhappy? She had a right to happiness. Frank would take her in his arms, fold her in his arms. He would save her.

*

She stood among the **swaying** crowd in the station at the **North Wall**. He held her hand and she knew that he was speaking to her, saying something about the **passage** over and over again. The station was full of soldiers with brown baggages. Through the wide doors of the **sheds** she **caught a glimpse** of the black mass of the boat, lying in beside the **quay** wall, with illumined **portholes**. She answered nothing, She felt her cheek pale and cold and, out of a **maze** of

---

**strut** [strʌt] stolzieren  **muse** [mjuːz] grübeln  **pitiful** ['pɪtɪfʊl] mitleiderregend  **laid its spell on the very quick of her being** schlug das Innerste ihres Wesens in ihren Bann  **commonplace** ['kɒmənpleɪs] alltäglich, banal  **sacrifices** Pl ['sækrɪfaɪsɪz] Opfer Pl, Aufopferung  **insistence** [ɪn'sɪstəns] Beharrlichkeit  **Derevaun Seraun** ['derəvɔːn ʃə'rɔːn] keltischer Kosename: „Unschuldiger Liebling"  **swaying** ['sweɪŋ] hin- und herwogend  **North Wall** Hafen in Dublin  **passage** ['pæsɪdʒ] Überfahrt, Schiffsreise  **shed** [ʃed] Schuppen  **catch a glimpse** [glɪmps] flüchtig sehen  **quay** [kiː] Kai  **porthole** ['pɔːthəʊl] Bullauge  **maze** [meɪz] Irrgarten, Verwirrung

**distress**, she prayed to God to direct her, to show her what was her duty. The boat blew a long **mournful** whistle into the **mist**. If she went, tomorrow she would be on the sea with Frank, steaming towards Buenos Ayres. Their passage had been booked. Could she still draw back after all he had done for her? Her distress awoke a **nausea** in her body and she kept moving her lips in silent **fervent** prayer.

A bell **clanged upon her heart**. She felt him seize her hand:

'Come!'

All the seas of the world **tumbled about her heart**. He was drawing her into them: he would **drown** her. She gripped with both hands at the iron **railing**.

'Come!'

No! No! No! It was impossible. Her hands **clutched** the iron in **frenzy**. Amid the seas she sent a cry of **angusih**.

'Eveline! Evvy!'

He rushed beyong the barrier and called to her to follow. He was shouted at to go on, but he still called to her. She set her white face to him, passive, like a helpless animal. Her eyes gave him no sign of love or farewell or recognition.

11. 3. 2000

---

**distress** [dɪsˈtres] Pein, Not   **mournful** [ˈmɔːnfʊl] traurig, düster
**mist** [mɪst] Nebel   **nausea** [ˈnɔːsjə] Brechreiz   **fervent** [ˈfɜːvənt]
inbrünstig   **clanged upon her heart** gellte gegen ihr Herz
**tumbled about her heart** stürzten auf sie ein   **drown s.o.** [draʊn] j-n
ertränken   **railing** [ˈreɪlɪŋ] Geländer   **clutch** [klʌtʃ] umklammern
**frenzy** [ˈfrenzɪ] wahnsinnige Erregung   **anguish** [ˈæŋgwɪʃ] Qual

# I Spy

*Graham Greene*

Charlie Stowe waited until he heard his mother snore before he got out of bed. Even then he moved with **caution** and tiptoed to the window. The front of the house was irregular, so that it was possible to see a light burning in his mother's room. But now all the windows were dark. A **search-light** passed across the sky, lighting the banks of cloud and **probing** the dark deep spaces between, seeking enemy **airships**. The wind blew from the sea, and Charlie Stowe could hear behind his mother's snores the beating of the waves. A **draught** through the **cracks** in the window-frame stirred his nightshirt. Charlie Stowe was frightened.

But the thought of the tobacconist's shop which his father kept down a dozen wooden stairs drew him on. He was twelve years old, and already boys at the County School **mocked** him because he had never smoked a cigarette. The packets were **piled twelve deep** below, Gold Flake and Players, **De Reszke, Abdulla**, Woodbines, and the little shop lay under a thin **haze** of **stale** smoke which would completely **disguise** his crime. That it was a crime to steal of his father's **stock** Charlie Stowe had no doubt, but he did not love his father; his father was unreal to him, a **wraith**, pale, thin, **indefinite**, who noticed him only **spasmodically** and left even punishment to his mother. For his mother he felt a passion-

---

**I Spy** Name eines kindlichen Ratespiels, ähnlich wie „Ich seh' etwas, was du nicht siehst …"  **caution** [ˈkɔːʃn] Vorsicht  **search-light** [ˈsɜːtʃlaɪt] (Such-)Scheinwerfer  **probe** [prəʊb] sondieren, absuchen  **airship** [ˈeəʃɪp] Luftschiff (im 1. Weltkrieg militärisch eingesetzt)  **draught** [drɑːft] Luftzug  **crack** [kræk] Riss, Spalt  **mock** verspotten  **piled twelve deep** zu einem Dutzend aufgestapelt  **De Reszke** [dəˈreskɪ], **Abdulla** [æbˈdʌlə] Zigarettenmarken  **haze** [heɪz] Dunst, Schleier  **stale** [steɪl] abgestanden, alt  **disguise** [dɪsˈgaɪz] tarnen  **stock** [stɒk] Vorrat, Lager  **wraith** [reɪθ] Gespenst  **indefinite** [ɪnˈdefɪnɪt] undeutlich  **spasmodically** [spæzˈmɒdɪkəlɪ] unregelmäßig

ate **demonstrative** love; her large **boisterous** presence and her noisy **charity** filled the world for him; from her speech he judged her the friend of everyone, from the **rector**'s wife to the 'dear Queen', except the '**Huns**', the monsters who **lurked** in Zeppelins in the clouds. But his father's **affection** and dislike were as indefinite as his **movements**. Tonight he had said he would be in Norwich, and yet you never knew. Charlie Stowe had no sense of safety as he crept down the wooden stairs. When they **creaked** he **clenched** his fingers on the collar of his nightshirt.

At the bottom of the stairs he came out quite suddenly into the little shop. It was too dark to see his way, and he did not dare touch the switch. For half a minute he sat in despair on the bottom step with his chin **cupped** in his hands. Then the regular movement of the searchlight was reflected through an upper window and the boy had time to **fix in memory** the pile of cigarettes, the counter, and the small hole under it. The footsteps of a policeman on the pavement made him grab the first packet to his hand and **dive for the hole**. A light shone along the floor and a hand tried the door, then the footsteps passed on, and Charlie **cowered** in the darkness.

At last he got his courage back by telling himself in his curiously **adult** way that if he were caught now there was nothing to be done about it, and he might as well have his smoke. He put a cigarette in his mouth and then remembered that he had no matches. For a while he dared not move. Three times the searchlight lit the shop, as he **muttered taunts and**

*Hohn*

---

**demonstrative** [dɪ'mɒnstrətɪv] überschwenglich    **boisterous** ['bɔɪstərəs] laut, ungestüm    **charity** ['tʃærɪtɪ] Herzensgüte    **rector** ['rektə] Pfarrer    **Hun** [hʌn] Hunne; (Schimpfwort für Deutscher) **lurk** [lɜːk] lauern    **affection** [ə'fekʃn] Liebe    **movements** Pl Handeln, Tun    **creak** [kriːk] knarren    **clench** [klentʃ] zusammenpressen    **cupped in his hands** in die Handteller gestützt    **fix in memory** sich einprägen    **dive for the hole** in dem Loch untertauchen    **cower** ['kaʊə] kauern    **adult** ['ædʌlt] erwachsen **mutter** ['mʌtə] murmeln    **taunts and encouragements** [tɔːnts] anpeitschende und ermutigende Worte

encouragements. 'May as well be hung for a sheep,' 'Cowardy, cowardy custard,' grown-up and childish **exhortations oddly** mixed. ⤳ *fi'ertoerni*

But as he moved he heard **footfalls** in the street, the sound of several men walking rapidly. Charlie Stowe was old enough to feel surprise that anybody was about. The footsteps came nearer, stopped; a key was turned in the shop door, a voice said: 'Let him in,' and then he heard his father, 'If you wouldn't mind being quiet, gentlemen. I don't want to wake up the family.' There was a note unfamiliar to Charlie in the undecided voice. A **torch** flashed and the electric **globe burst into blue light**. The boy held his breath; he wondered whether his father would hear his heart beating, and he **clutched** his nightshirt **tightly** and prayed, 'O God, don't let me be caught.' Through a crack in the counter he could see his father where he stood, one hand held to his high stiff collar, between two men in **bowler hats** and **belted mackintoshes**. They were strangers.

'Have a cigarette,' his father said in a voice dry as a biscuit. One of the men shook his head. 'It wouldn't do, not when we are **on duty**. Thank you **all the same**.' He spoke gently, but without kindness: Charlie Stowe thought his father must be ill.

'Mind if I put a few in my pocket?' Mr Stowe asked, and when the man nodded he lifted a pile of Gold Flake and Players from a shelf and **caressed** the packets with the tips of his fingers.

---

**May as well be hung** (= hanged) **for a sheep** (as for a lamb.) etwa: Wenn schon, denn schon!   **Cowardy, cowardy custard.** etwa: Wer fürchtet sich vorm schwarzen Mann?   **exhortation** [egzɔː'teɪʃn] Ermunterung, Zureden   **odd** [ɒd] seltsam   **footfall** ['fʊtfɔːl] Schritt   **torch** [tɔːtʃ] Taschenlampe   **the ... globe burst into blue light** die ... Kugellampe flammte blau auf   **clutch** [klʌtʃ] packen, drücken   **tight** [taɪt] fest   **bowler hat** ['bəʊlə] steifer Hut, „Melone"   **belted** ['beltɪd] gegürtet   **mackintosh** ['mækɪntɒʃ] Regenmantel   **on duty** ['djuːtɪ] im Dienst   **all the same** trotzdem   **caress** [kə'res] liebkosen, streicheln

'Well,' he said, 'there's nothing to be done about it, and I may as well have my smokes.' For a moment Charlie Stowe feared discovery, his father stared round the shop so thoroughly; he might have been seeing it for the first time. 'It's a good little business,' he said, 'for those that like it. The wife will sell out, I suppose. Else the neighbours'll be **wrecking** it. Well, you want to be off. **A stitch in time.** I'll get my coat.'

'One of us'll come with you, if you don't mind,' said the stranger gently. *the coat*

'You needn't trouble. It's on the **peg** here. There, I'm all ready.'

The other man said in an **embarrassed** way, 'Don't you want to speak to your wife?' The thin voice was decided, 'Not me. **Never do today what you can put off till tomorrow.** She'll have her chance later, won't she?'

'Yes, yes,' one of the strangers said and he became very cheerful and encouraging. 'Don't you worry too much. **While there's life …**' and suddenly his father tried to laugh.

When the door had closed Charlie Stowe tiptoed upstairs and got into bed. He wondered why his father had left the house again so late at night and who the strangers were. Surprise and **awe** kept him for a little while awake. It was as if a familiar photograph had stepped from the frame to **reproach him with neglect**. He remembered how his father had held tight to his collar and **fortified** himself with proverbs, and he thought for the first time that, while his mother was boisterous and **kindly**, his father was very like

---

**wreck** [rek] zertrümmern, kaputtmachen   **A stitch in time (saves nine).** etwa: Was du heute kannst besorgen …   **peg** Haken
**embarrassed** [ɪmˈbærəst] verlegen   **Never do today …** scherzhafte Umkehrung von: **Never put off tomorrow what you can do today.**   **While there is life (there is hope.)** Man hofft, solange man lebt.   **awe** [ɔː] Furcht, Scheu   **to reproach him with neglect** [rɪˈprəʊtʃ, nɪˈglekt] um ihm Missachtung vorzuwerfen
**fortify** [ˈfɔːtɪfaɪ] stärken, Mut machen   **kindly** = kind

himself, doing things in the dark which frightened him. It would have pleased him to go down to this father and tell him that he loved him, but he could hear through the window the quick steps going away. He was alone in the house with his mother, and he fell asleep.

10. 3. 2006 (3x)

# My Financial Career

*Stephen Leacock*

When I go into a bank I get **rattled**. The clerks rattle me; the **wickets** rattle me; the sight of the money rattles me; everything rattles me.

The moment I cross the **threshold** of a bank and attempt to **transact** business there, I become an **irresponsible** idiot.

I knew this beforehand, but my salary had been raised to fifty dollars a month and I felt that the bank was the only place for it.

So I **shambled** in and looked **timidly** round at the clerks. I had an idea that a person about to open an **account** must **needs** consult the manager.

I went up to a wicket marked '**Accountant**'. The accountant was a tall, cool devil. The very sight of him rattled me. **My voice was sepulchral.**

'Can I see the manager?' I said, and added **solemnly**, 'alone'. I don't know why I said 'alone'.

'Certainly', said the accountant, and fetched him.

The manager was a grave, calm man. I held my fifty-six dollars **clutched** in a **crumpled** ball in my pocket.

'Are you the manager?' I said. God knows I didn't doubt it. 'Yes,' he said.

'Can I see you,' I asked, 'alone?' I didn't want to say 'alone' again, but without it the thing seemend **self-evident**.

---

rattle F ['rætl] nervös machen, aus der Fassung bringen   **wicket** ['wɪkɪt] Schalterfenster   **threshold** ['θreʃhəʊld] Schwelle   **transact** [træn'zækt] abwickeln   **irresponsible** [ɪrɪs'pɒnsəbl] unzurechnungsfähig   **shamble** ['ʃæmbl] torkeln   **timid** ['tɪmɪd] ängstlich, zaghaft   **account** [ə'kaʊnt] Konto   **needs** [niːdz] unbedingt   **accountant** [ə'kaʊntənt] „Kontenführung"; Buchhalter   **My voice was sepulchral.** [sɪ'pʌlkrəl] Ich sprach mit Grabesstimme.   **solemn** ['sɒləm] feierlich   **clutch** [klʌtʃ] umklammern   **crumple** ['krʌmpl] zerknüllen   **self-evident** offensichtlich

The manager looked at me **in some alarm**. He felt that I had an awful secret to **reveal**.

'Come in here,' he said, and led the way to a private room. He turned the key in the lock.

'We are safe from interruption here,' he said, 'sit down.'

We both sat down and looked at each other. I found no voice to speak.

'You are one of **Pinkerton**'s men, I **presume**,' he said.

He had **gathered** from my mysterious manner that I was a detective. I knew what he was thinking, and it made me worse.

'No, not from Pinkertons's, I said, seeming to **imply** that I came from a **rival agency**.

'To tell the truth,' I went on, as if I had been **prompted** to lie about it, 'I am not a detective at all. I have come to open an account. I intend to keep all my money in this bank.'

The manager looked **relieved** but still serious: he concluded now that I was a son of Baron **Rothschild** or a young **Gould**.

'A large account, I suppose,' he said.

'**Fairly** large,' I whispered. 'I propose to **deposit** fifty-six dollars now and fifty dollars a month regularly.'

The manager got up and opened the door. He called to the accountant.

'Mr Montgomery,' he said unkindly loud, 'this gentleman is opening an account, he will deposit fifty-six dollars. Good morning.'

---

**in some alarm** [ə'lɑ:m] einigermaßen beunruhigt   **reveal** [rɪ'vi:l] enthüllen, offenbaren   **Pinkerton** ['pɪŋkətən] Gründer e-r amer. Detektivorganisation, die heute noch besteht   **presume** [prɪ'zju:m] vermuten   **gather** ['gæðə] folgern   **imply** [ɪm'plaɪ] andeuten   **rival agency** ['raɪvəl 'eɪdʒənsɪ] Konkurrenzagentur   **prompt** [prɒmpt] bewegen, veranlassen   **relieved** [rɪ'li:vd] erleichtert   **Rothschild** ['rɒθtʃaɪld] internationale Finanzdynastie   **Gould** [gu:ld] amer. Finanzier (1836–92)   **fairly** ['feəlɪ] ziemlich   **deposit** [dɪ'pɒzɪt] einzahlen

I rose.

A big iron door stood open at the side of the room.

'Good morning,' I said and stepped into the safe.

'Come out,' said the manager coldly, and showed me the other way.

I went up to the accountant's wicket and **poked** the ball of money at him with a quick **convulsive** movement as if I were doing a **conjuring trick**.

My face was **ghastly pale**.

'Here,' I said, 'deposit it.' The tone of the words seemed to mean, 'Let us do this painful thing **while the fit is on us**.'

He took the money and gave it to another clerk.

He made me write the sum on a **slip** and sign my name in a book. I no longer knew what I was doing. The bank swam before my eyes.

'Is it deposited?' I asked in a **hollow**, vibrating voice.

'It is,' said the accountant.

'Then I want **to draw a cheque**.'

My idea was to draw out six dollars of it for present use. Someone gave me a cheque-book through a wicket and someone else began telling me how to write it out. The people in the bank had the impression that I was an invalid millionaire. I wrote something on the cheque and **thrust** it in at the clerk. He looked at it.

'What! are you drawing it all out again?' he asked in surprise. Then I realised that I had written fifty-six instead of six. I was too far gone to **reason** now. I had a feeling it was im-

---

**poke** [pəʊk] stoßen, schieben   **convulsive** [kənˈvʌlsɪv] krampfhaft
**conjuring trick** [ˈkʌndʒərɪŋ] Zauberkunststück   **ghastly pale**
[ˈgɑːstlɪ] totenbleich   **while the fit is on us** solange der Anfall an-
hält   **slip** [slɪp] Zettel   **hollow** [ˈhɒləʊ] hohl   **draw a cheque** [tʃek]
e-n Scheck einlösen   **thrust** [θrʌst] stoßen, schieben   **reason** [ˈriːzn]
vernünftig diskutieren

possible to explain the thing. All the clerks had stopped writing to look at me.

**Reckless** with misery, I **made a plunge**.

'Yes, the whole thing.'

'You want to **withdraw** your money from the bank?'

'Every cent of it.'

'Are you not going to deposit any more?' said the clerk, astonished.

'Never.'

An idiot hope **struck** me that they might think something had **insulted** me while I was writing the cheque and that I had changed my mind. I made a **wretched** attempt to look like a man with a fearfully **quick temper**.

The clerk prepared to pay the money.

'How will you have it?' he said.

'What?'

'How will you have it?'

'Oh'—I **caught his meaning** and answered without even trying to think—'in fifties.'

He gave me a fifty-dollar bill.

'And the six?' he asked dryly.

'In sixes,' I said.

He gave it me and I rushed out.

As the big door swung behind me I caught the echo of a roar of laughter that went up to the ceiling of the bank. Since then I **bank** no more. I keep my money **in cash** in my trousers pocket and my **savings** in silver dollars in a sock.

11. 3. 2006

---

reckless ['reklɪs] rücksichtslos, bedenkenlos   **make a plunge** [plʌndʒ] die Flucht nach vorn antreten   **withdraw** [wɪð'drɔ:] abheben   **struck me** von **strike** kam mir in den Sinn   **insult** [ɪn'sʌlt] beleidigen   **wretched** ['retʃɪd] kläglich   **quick temper** hitziges Temperament   **caught his meaning** von **catch** verstand, was er meinte   **bank** [bæŋk] Bankgeschäfte machen   **in cash** [kæʃ] bar **savings** ['seɪvɪŋz] Ersparnisse

# Kurzbiografien

**Budd Schulberg** (1914) wurde als Sohn eines Filmproduzenten in New York City geboren. Er verbrachte seine Jugend in Hollywood, wo er das Leben der großen Stars aus nächster Nähe beobachten konnte. Die meisten seiner Romane und Kurzgeschichten handeln von der glitzernden Welt des Showbusiness.

**Fredric Brown** (1906–1972) war von Haus aus Journalist. Er machte sich eine vignettenhaft knappe Spielart der Sciencefiction Story zu eigen, in der ausgeklügelte Überraschungseffekte mit geschliffener Eleganz dargeboten werden.

**Irwin Shaw** (1913–1984), geboren in Brooklyn (New York), ist ein international bekannter Autor von Erzählungen, Theaterstücken und Filmdrehbüchern. In vielen seiner Werke ("The Young Lions", "Bread upon the Waters" etc.) steht hinter der weltmännischen Leichtigkeit und Eleganz der Erzählweise ein leidenschaftlicher Protest gegen Krieg und soziale Benachteiligung.

**Angelica Gibbs** wurde in New York City geboren. Als Schwester von Wolcott Gibbs, der als langjähriger Redakteur den 1925 gegründeten "New Yorker" mitgestaltete, veröffentlichte sie zwischen 1931 und 1953 zahlreiche Erzählungen und Aufsätze in dieser gesellschaftskritischen und satirischen Wochenzeitschrift.

**Henry Slesar** (1927–2002) war ursprünglich Werbefachmann, bevor er zu schreiben begann. Sein galliger Humor am Rande schauerlicher Abgründe ist das Wasserzeichen seiner rund 500 Kurzgeschichten, von denen ein Drittel dem Bereich phantastischer Zukunftsvisionen zuzurechnen ist.

**Ray Bradbury** (1920) ist einer der bekanntesten Vertreter amerikanischer Sciencefiction. Seinen kürzeren und längeren Erzählungen, deren bekanntester Titel "Fahrenheit 451" ist, liegt oft eine gesellschaftskritische Haltung zugrunde.

**John Collier** (1901–1980), ein in London geborener Amerikaner, ist vor allem wegen seiner Kurzgeschichten bekannt, in denen sich skurrile Phantasie und ironisch servierter Horror zu einer intellektuell gefälligen Mischung vereinen.

**James Thurber** (1894–1961) stammte aus Columbus (Ohio). Als Humorist und Zeichner illustrierte er seine Bücher mit eigenen Karikaturen. Um seine skeptischen Lebensweisheiten anschaulich zu machen, bediente er sich unter anderem der Fabel. Sein Werk ist voll komischer Antihelden, die mit dem modernen Leben nicht zurechtkommen.

**Arnold Bennett** (1867–1931) wurde im Industriegebiet von Mittelengland geboren. In den meisten seiner Romane, unter denen "The Old Wives' Tale" als Klassiker des englischen Realismus gilt, beschäftigt er sich mit dem Alltag des Töpferlandes von Staffordshire und den Schicksalen seiner einfachen Menschen.

**W. Somerset Maugham** (1874–1965), geboren in Paris, wuchs in England auf, wo er Medizin studierte, ohne je den Beruf des Mediziners auszuüben. Später lebte er, von zahlreichen Reisen abgesehen, an der französischen Riviera. Seiner kosmopolitischen Natur entsprechend, bildet eine internationale Gesellschaft den Hintergrund seiner Werke, deren Personenschilderungen an die klinische Diagnose eines Arztes erinnern. (Autobiogr. Roman "Of Human Bondage", Kurzgeschichtensammlungen, Gesellschaftsdramen).

**Morley Callaghan** (1903–1990) wurde in Kanada geboren und lebte in den zwanziger Jahren zusammen mit Hemingway in Paris. Er schrieb Romane und Kurzgeschichten, die in ihrer getreuen Schilderung von Alltagssituationen und ihrer subtilen Analyse von Empfindungen an die Erzählkunst eines Tschechow erinnern.

**Frank Tuohy** (1925) wählte den Beruf des Universitätsdozenten. Im Rahmen des British Council wirkte er als Kultur- und Literaturinterpret seines Landes in Finnland, Brasilien, Polen und Japan. Er zeichnet sich vor allem durch seine Kurzgeschichten aus, denen die bekannte Autorin Muriel Spark bescheinigte, sie hätten einen „eingebauten Lügen- und Snobdetektor" zur Entlarvung der menschlichen Seele.

**James Joyce** (1882–1941) wurde in Dublin geboren und in einem Jesuitenkolleg erzogen. Schon früh brach er mit der Kirche, verließ die Enge seiner Heimat und führte bis zu seinem Tod ein unstetes Leben, dessen Hauptstationen Paris, Triest und Zürich waren. Joyce ist einer der großen Neuerer. Mit seinem neue Bewusstseinsbereiche erschließenden „inneren Monolog" ("Dubliner", "Ulysses") und seinem kühnen Versuch, bis ins Unterbewusste vorzudringen ("Finnegan's Wake") hat er die heutige Literatur entscheidend beeinflusst.

**Graham Greene** (1904–1991), geboren in Südengland, ist einer der berühmtesten englischen Erzähler dieses Jahrhunderts. Er trat 1926 zum Katholizismus über, arbeitete im Zweiten Weltkrieg für das Britische Außenministerium und lebte längere Zeit in Westafrika und Mittelamerika. Der Hauptteil seines Werkes ("The Power and the Glory", "The Heart of the Matter", "A Burnt-out Case") spürt dem Geheimnis menschlicher Schuld nach und sucht Antwort auf die Frage, wie der von Gott abgefallene Mensch die göttliche Gnade erlangen kann.

**Stephen Leacock** (1869–1944) ist kanadischer Herkunft. Von Haus aus Politologe, wurde er verhältnismäßig spät Schriftsteller. Er ist bekannt wegen seines robusten, oft überschäumenden Humors, der ihn in den Augen mancher Kritiker in die Nähe Mark Twains rückt.